LOVE
at
HOME

Insights from *the* Lives *of* Latter-day Prophets

LOVE *at* HOME

ALONZO L. GASKILL
STEVEN T. LINFORD

CFI
An imprint of Cedar Fort, Inc.
Springville, Utah

ISBN 13: 978-1-4621-1271-5

LIBRARY OF CONGRESS CATALOGING-IN-PUBLICATION DATA

Gaskill, Alonzo L., author.
Love at home : insights from the lives of latter-day prophets / Alonzo L. Gaskill, Steven T. Linford.
    pages cm
Includes bibliographical references and index.
ISBN 978-1-4621-1271-5 (alk. paper)
1. Marriage--Religious aspects--Church of Jesus Christ of Latter-day Saints. 2. Domestic relations.
I. Linford, Steven T., author. II. Title.

BX8643.M36G37 2013
248.4'89332--dc23

2013018036

Published by CFI, an imprint of Cedar Fort, Inc.
2373 W. 700 S., Springville, UT 84663
Distributed by Cedar Fort, Inc., www.cedarfort.com

Cover design by Shawnda T. Craig
Cover design © 2013 Lyle Mortimer
Edited and typeset by Emily S. Chambers

Printed in the United States of America

10 9 8 7 6 5 4 3 2 1

Dedication

In gratitude for prophets and apostles—ancient and modern—who have taught us through word and example how to develop marriages and families worthy to endure throughout all eternity!
—ALG

To Melanie, my beautiful wife, whom I love with all my heart.
—STL

Acknowledgments

We gratefully acknowledge the invaluable aid of our research assistant, Marissa Widdison. Her many hours of work on this project—mining for quotes, organizing materials, acting as a sounding board, and reviewing drafts—have improved our work significantly. She is an exemplary daughter of God, for whom we have great respect and admiration. Marissa, thank you!

Contents

Introduction

*"Wherefore, . . . thou shalt give heed unto all his words
and commandments which he shall give unto you as he
receiveth them, walking in all holiness before me; For his
word ye shall receive, as if from mine own mouth, in all
patience and faith." —Doctrine and Covenants 21:4–5*

THESE ARE SUCH CURIOUS TIMES. WHILE WE HAVE MUCH
sin and temptation in our day, President Gordon B. Hinckley never tired of pointing out that this is the most glorious
time in the history of the world. So many opportunities and blessings enrich our lives, bring comfort and ease, and guide us on the
path to exaltation.

Every individual, and each family, has dark days—trials that
seem almost insurmountable. As Latter-day Saints—having such
high ideals of how home, family, and relationships should be—we
may at times wonder why our lives never seem to meet the ideal.
We may forget that the prophets and their families face many of
the same challenges you and I do: children stray, financial crises hit,
health challenges come, or a loved one dies. Prophets and apostles
are not immune from these same trials, tests, and difficulties.

While we look to God and Christ as our examples, we know
that the living prophets and apostles are our mortal models of
how to live. They not only give us God's word in these latter days,
they also teach us, by their examples, how to face the challenges
of the mortal experience. We can learn much from their lives and
experiences.

Over the years, Steve and I have amassed quite a corpus of personal experiences the Brethren have shared in various venues—experiences that testify that they have lived lives like ours, with good days and bad, with triumphs and tragedies. Their frank and open sharing of these experiences has provided many opportunities for you and me to learn how to gracefully handle opposition and strengthen our relationships with those we love, particularly during the trying times. We have entitled this small book *Love at Home* because it is our belief that this is what the Brethren have offered us. Their closeness to God, and their spiritual maturity, enables them to give us healing counsel that, if applied, can change our lives and our relationships.

The Lord has commanded us to receive His word from the living prophets and apostles "as if from [His] own mouth, in all patience and faith" (Doctrine and Covenants 21:5). Each of us is blessed to live in the dispensation of the fulness of times, wherein those words are readily accessible. We have found rich blessings from applying the counsel and example of the holy prophets. Following their words and way helps fortify our faith, renew our hope, and give us the strength and encouragement to press forward. Mother Teresa used to say, "Take whatever God gives and give whatever He takes, with a big smile."[1] The Brethren are such wonderful examples of how to do this.

Of course, Christ is ultimately the source of all *true* healing. As we access the Atonement through our prayers and obedience and, when necessary, through our repentance, we will be filled with His love, His grace, and His strength—which drives away all doubt, fear, and discouragement. It is our sincere hope that the contents of this small book will lead couples and families to the Lord, who has the power to "lift up the hands which hang down, and [to] strengthen the feeble knees" (Doctrine and Covenants 81:5). In writing this, it is our earnest desire that members of the Church will learn from the examples of Christ's earthly representatives how to gracefully and successful traverse the obstacle-strewn path that is mortality, and thereby regain the presence of the Father.

1

Counseling *with* Each Other *& the* Lord

"Come now therefore, and let us take counsel together." —Nehemiah 6:7

THE SEVENTEENTH-CENTURY ENGLISH POET JOHN DONNE penned these immortal words: "No man is an Island, entire of it self [*sic*]; every man is a piece of the Continent, a part of the main."[2] How often we forget this timeless truth. Each of us has been divinely endowed with the agency to make choices. However, once a man and woman kneel at an altar to enter into the new and everlasting covenant of marriage (Doctrine and Covenants 131:2), a family is established, and the actions and decisions of each member of that family ever affect the others. Thus, counseling with our spouse, in concert with inquiring of the Lord, is a paramount practice for those who hope to be guided down the specific path the Lord has in mind for our specific life, our specific companionship, and our specific family.

It is certainly no coincidence that the Lord in New Testament times sent the Seventy out two by two (Luke 10:1), as He has missionaries in this dispensation (Doctrine and Covenants 42:6). "Two heads are better than one," as the proverbial saying goes. To avoid the counsel of one's spouse—or more important, the Lord—is to court danger and to chart a reckless path almost sure to lead us somewhere other than where the Lord intended.

President Eyring had a seminally life-changing experience early in his career that illustrates the need for husbands and wives to counsel with each other, to inquire of the Lord, and to follow diligently the guidance of the Holy Spirit—even in matters which are *seemingly* temporal.

In 1971, Henry Eyring was a tenured professor at Stanford University and was also serving as the bishop of one of the Stanford wards. He was excelling at work and was serving in a Church calling that brought him a great deal of spiritual satisfaction. It seemed an idyllic time in their lives—until his wife awoke in the middle of the night with some unexpected questions.

"Are you sure you are doing the right thing with your life?" she asked.

Puzzled by both the question and the hour of the night at which she chose to ask it, he responded, "What do you mean?"

Sister Eyring's next question seemed stranger than the first: "Couldn't you be doing studies for Neal Maxwell?" (At the time, Elder Maxwell was serving as the newly appointed commissioner of the Church Educational System.) Bishop Eyring was puzzled by the suggestion. He didn't know Commissioner Maxwell, and he had no reason to assume that Brother Maxwell needed the assistance of a tenured business professor in the commissioner's office. Nevertheless, Sister Eyring felt that perhaps her husband could be doing more to change lives.

Bishop Eyring's reply to his wife's middle-of-the-night questions was simply this: "Doing studies for Neal Maxwell—at my stage of my career?" *Studies* were what students did. He was a professor. The suggestion made no sense to him.

Sister Eyring paused and then simply asked him if he would pray about it. Of course, they had been married long enough for him to know that ignoring his wife's counsel was never wise. So he immediately got out of bed, knelt down, and offered a prayer. He described the experience as follows: "I got no answer, and I felt terrific about it because I didn't want to go anywhere."

The next evening Bishop Eyring was holding his weekly

bishopric meeting, and the voice of the Spirit came to him, rebuking him for treating lightly his wife's questions, which he realized had been promptings from the Holy Ghost. "You don't know what way is up in your career," he was told. "If you ever get another job offer, you bring it to me."

Bishop Eyring was unsettled by the revelatory experience he had just received. He quickly went home and said to his wife, "We have a problem." He was worried that he had made a mistake because he has passed up several job offers that had come to him while he was a professor at Stanford. He hadn't prayed over any of them, because he was entirely content with where he was and with what he was doing. He was sobered by what the Spirit had taught him. Humbled, he began praying about his future and what the Lord would have him do.

Less than a week after Sister Eyring's surprise late-night questions, the Eyrings received an unexpected call from Commissioner Maxwell. He asked Bishop Eyring to come to Salt Lake to meet with him. He flew out the next day and when they met, the first words out of Commissioner Maxwell's mouth were, "I'd like to ask you to be the president of Ricks College." Even Sister Eyring's promptings and the Spirit's rather strong rebuke to Bishop Eyring had not prepared the two of them for this. They were blindsided by the request. Brother Eyring told Commissioner Maxwell that he would need to pray about this before he could give an answer.

Without saying yes or no, Bishop Eyring headed back to California, pleading with the Lord for an answer. This decision seemed contrary to all he was doing with his life. Leave Stanford University for Ricks College? He could almost hear his colleagues saying, "Hal, you've got to be kidding! What are you thinking? It's a junior college! And who is 'Rick'?"

But as he prayed, an answer came. "I heard a voice so faint that I hadn't paid attention to it," he recalled. "The voice said, 'It's my school.'" Bishop Eyring called Commissioner Maxwell and said, "I'm coming." While it seemed an almost insane decision, he would see the Lord's hand manifest many times because of that decision to obey the promptings given to both him and his wife.[3]

President Eyring's experience teaches a number of principles. First of all, we learn that at times in our lives God will bring revelation to us and for us but does so through our spouse. The experience of Bishop John Wells, formerly a member of the Presiding Bishopric, also illustrates this truth.

A son of Bishop Wells had been killed in Emigration Canyon in a railroad accident, and sometime after his death he appeared to his grieving mother. After consoling her, he informed her that he had been trying to manifest himself to his father but had been unsuccessful, as his father was so consumed in his duties that he was unable to receive the angelic ministrant. Thus, the Wellses' son had appeared to his mother and asked that she convey the revelation to Bishop Wells.[4] Even in revelation, husband and wife must become "one" (Genesis 2:24; John 17:21).

A second principle illustrated in the Eyring's experience is this: as companionships and families, prior to any major decisions, we must always petition the Lord to manifest His will. When we enter the Lord's holy house and covenant to live the law of consecration, we promise from that day forward that our lives are not our own, nor are our education, careers, and life-paths. Therefore, we must constantly seek God's guidance and direction that our lives might be lived in accordance with His will.

Elder Richard L. Evans of the Council of the Twelve taught this regarding the importance of counseling with others:

> My beloved brethren and sisters, may we take counsel with each other. There is safety in counsel: counsel with our children, with the family, with our friends, with our Father in heaven, and [do] not attempt to live life alone and to make the decisions alone, but to strengthen each other, and encourage each other, and go forward and do what there is to be done and follow the living leadership as the prophet interprets for us the great principles and commandments of all time.[5]

On another occasion, Elder Evans wrote, "No man is smart

enough to know all the answers. No man is so wise that he cannot benefit by talking things out with others. (There was a great council in heaven, before the world was.) And don't forget to talk things out with the Lord."[6] The fact remains, marriages where the husband and wife fail to counsel with each other and the Lord tend to fail!

Quotes to Contemplate

"Hearken now unto my voice, I will give thee counsel, and God shall be with thee."

—*Exodus 18:19*

"God does notice us, and he watches over us. But it is usually through another mortal that he meets our needs."

—*Spencer W. Kimball*

"In the home it is a partnership with husband and wife equally yoked together, sharing in decisions, always working together."

—*Boyd K. Packer*

2

Supporting Each Other
as Husband *&* Wife

*"Bear ye one another's burdens, and so fulfill
the law of Christ." —Galatians 6:2*

THE STORY HAS BEEN TOLD OF A YOUNG, NINETEENTH-century Brit by the name of Samuel Plimsoll who had an inordinate fascination with the carrying capacity of boats. As he watched cargo loaded onto and off of ships, he observed that each vessel had a maximum capacity it could hold, regardless of the space available within its hulls. Plimsoll came to discover that if a ship exceeded its weight limit, it would likely sink. Because of his discovery, ship builders began to draw a line (known as the "Plimsoll line") on the hull of ships they built. When the cargo was loaded, the weight lowered the ship deeper into the water. Once the "Plimsoll line" on the hull reached the surface of the water, the loading ceased even if there was additional room for cargo. When the weight-bearing limit was reached, another ship had to be brought in to carry the load the previous ship could not safely bear. As a result of the "Plimsoll line," British deaths at sea were reduced dramatically.[7]

Like ships, each of us has our own "carrying capacity." Our ability to shoulder the loads and burdens of life varies from year to year and perhaps even from day to day. The Lord places others around us to shoulder those burdens so that we don't sink as we

9

sail the turbulent waters of mortality. Truly, each person has his or her own "Plimsoll line" that is representative of the burdens that they can shoulder. When we see our spouse or a loved one sinking because of the weight of life's burdens, we must assist them through off-loading some of that which is burdening them, lest the weight they are carrying overcomes them, causing them to drown in the sea of troubles common to all mankind.

A review of the lives of the Brethren offers numerous illustrations of this principle in action. For example, after years of noticing how President and Sister Faust seemed constantly aware of each other's needs, Elder Jeffrey R. Holland observed that they had an "unusual relationship and romance." President Faust was considerate, gentle, and attentive to his sweet wife. It was simple things, like walking at her pace when she was by his side, or taking her arm as they strolled together. Elder Holland noticed that, if in a public setting, President Faust would always look around for Sister Faust—just to make sure she was okay.

Of her, Elder Holland pointed out, "She . . . is absolutely, flat-out adoring of this man. He is twenty-eight feet tall in her eyes. If you ask her how he did with a talk, she lights up like a Christmas tree. If his name is even mentioned, she looks like 220 volts just got plugged in."

Much of his success has been possible because of the "unqualified, uncompromised, unlimited adoration and support and love and loyalty of his wife; and she has had exactly the same kind of support from him." Elder Holland pointed out, this wasn't "just handed to them from on high; I think that kind of relationship and romance has to be worked at and earned."[8]

As evidence of his awareness of how Sister Faust had carried many of his burdens, President Faust once noted, "I'm grateful to have Sister Faust here with me. When we decided to get married, I told her that I needed her help and that I needed to get more schooling and would appreciate her support, and I can honestly say that she gave that support and much, much more and made it possible for me to do some of the things that I've done in my life. I guess

I should say to you that marriage involves having a helpmeet, and Sister Faust has been very much my best helpmeet."[9] Similarly, after receiving his call to the holy apostleship, Elder Faust paid this tribute to his sweetheart: "No one could have a more supportive, understanding, and loving companion through all the circumstances of my life, both professionally and ecclesiastically. That's just the woof and warp of that wonderful woman."[10]

The Fausts were not occasional helpmeets to each other. Their lives were constantly saturated in concern for the welfare and well-being of each other. President Faust's secretary, Margaret Bury, observed that upon leaving the office each day, his attention would visibly shift to "What can I do now for Ruth?" When he was home, he and Ruth would turn their focus toward their family.[11] As Elder Holland noted, this approach to life and love was not "just handed to them from on high." The Fausts developed these attributes individually and as a companionship because they loved each other, and because they wanted a happy, godly marriage. No doubt, their accomplishment is within the grasp of *any* faithful Latter-day Saint couple who wish to experience the joys President and Sister Faust found in their relationship with each other. After years of observing many couples, Elder Robert D. Hales shared the following about supportive couples who have maintained strong and vital marriages, and have remained true to their temple covenants: "These couples think of one another before self. They grow together, and not apart, as they serve one another, love one another, care for one another, and communicate together with the Lord in prayer. . . . They cultivate a thoughtful, considerate spirit and love one another always. In so doing, they lift each other to high ground and strengthen one another in their determination to stay there together."[12]

At times, all of us sink below our personal "Plimsoll line" and need the support of a loving spouse or friend. Likewise, we too can off-load some of the burden carried by those whom we love and thereby help another to endure the difficulties that inevitably come. During those trying times, if a couple comes together and buoys each other up, they will continue to move forward in their relationship and in the challenges that constitute so much of this life. Of course, the Lord will help—not necessarily by removing the burdens, but often by strengthening us so that we can carry those burdens (see Mosiah 24:21). As the hymn states, "No waters can swallow the ship where lies / The Master of ocean and earth and skies."[13] Christ might not always calm the storm, but He can calm the heart of the person who is experiencing it by whispering "Peace, peace, be still" to our troubled souls. Our role, when others are weighed down, is described well by President Spencer W. Kimball, who reminded us, "God does notice us, and he watches over us. But it is usually through another mortal that he meets our needs."[14]

Prophets, ancient and modern, have spoken of the obligations we have to help lift up those who are weighed down, and they have promised us rich blessings as we do so. For example, in the book of Mosiah, Alma informs us that we should be "willing to bear one another's burdens, that they may be light; . . . and . . . willing to mourn with those that mourn; yea, and comfort those that stand in need of comfort" (Mosiah 18:8–9). As baptized members of the Church, this is our charge. But the Lord has also promised that as we so bless others, we too will be blessed—and He will "pour out his Spirit more abundantly upon" us (Mosiah 18:10). Like those of old who "clapped their hands for joy" (Mosiah 18:11) when this opportunity was presented to them, you and I must look to "lift up the hands which hang down, and strengthen the feeble knees" (Doctrine and Covenants 81:5; Hebrews 12:12). This will bless others. But, ultimately, we will be blessed equally for lightening the burden of another. That is an eternal law! Elder Jeffrey R. Holland has said, "One of the great purposes of true love is to help each other in [difficult] times. No one ought to have to face such trials alone. We can endure almost anything if we have someone at our side who truly loves us, who is easing the burden and lightening the load."[15]

In the lives of the prophets and apostles, we see example after example of tremendous support given and received in marriage. We find inspiring examples of these couples enduring tremendous trials and hardships—such as losing a child to death, suffering with sickness and disease, experiencing financial hardships, bearing heavy responsibilities, and so forth. Where so many relationships collapse under pressures such as these, we find the living prophets and apostles drawing closer to their spouses in such circumstances, supporting each other, and relying on each other for help and strength. Couples who support each other and work together are able to do marvelous things! Elder Bruce R. McConkie taught the following about righteous men and women. "The Lord never sends apostles and prophets and righteous men to minister to his people without placing a woman of like spiritual stature at their sides. . . . The exaltation of the one is dependent upon that of the other."[16] As we work to support one another, side by side, we will successfully face *all* of life's challenges together and "will lift each other to high ground and strengthen one another in [our] determination to stay there together."[17] As we do so, we will be blessed with the strength to endure anything, because we have someone by our side who truly loves us, and who seeks to ease our burdens and lighten our load.[18]

Quotes to Contemplate

"Love is defined by the Lord, elevates, protects, respects, and enriches another. It motivates one to make sacrifices for another."
—*Richard G. Scott*

"Rejoice with them that do rejoice, and weep with them that weep."
—*Romans 12:15*

"God has not called us to see through each other, but to see each other through."

—*Author Unknown*

"Our prayers for others flow more easily than those for ourselves. This shows we are made to live by charity."
—*C. S. Lewis*

3

Facing *the* Storms *of* Life

*"In the world ye shall have tribulation; but be of good
cheer; I have overcome the world." —John 16:33*

IN THE FOURTH CHAPTER OF THE GOSPEL OF MARK, WE LEARN
of the disciples' treacherous crossing of the Sea of Galilee. While
Jesus slept, a "great storm of wind" arose, and "the waves beat
into the ship, so that it was . . . full" of water to the point of sinking
(Mark 4:37). Peter and the other brethren aboard feared greatly for
their lives. No doubt, as they stared death in the face, each felt a
sense that all that they held dear was about to be stripped from their
grasp. Jesus's words of rebuke to them ("Why are ye so fearful? How
is it that ye have no faith?" [Mark 4:40]) highlight the desperation
and doubt that had enveloped them.

Similarly, the faith of nineteenth-century Chicago native Mary
Ann Baker was greatly challenged when her parents died rather
unexpectedly from a respiratory ailment that would shortly claim
the life of her only brother. Having just lost their parents, when
Mary Ann and her sister heard the news that their much beloved
brother had passed while recuperating out of state, they were dev-
astated. Adding to their grief were their circumstances; their health
and finances wouldn't allow them to have their brother's body
returned to Chicago for a proper burial.

While the Bakers were faithful Christians, the premature death of Mary's parents and brother—coupled with her own poor health and destitute circumstances—caused her to doubt God's loving nature. To her sister, she confided her newfound belief that "God does not care for me or mine." She added, "This particular manifestation of what they call 'divine providence' is unworthy of a God of love." In her hour of despair, Mary puzzled, "I have always tried to believe on Christ and give the Master a consecrated life, but this is more than I can bear. What have I done to deserve this? What have I left undone that God should wreak His vengeance upon me in this way?"[19]

Like Mary Ann Baker and the first-century disciples of Christ, many of us know intimately how intense, terrifying, and even perilous storms of life can become. When their ship was about to sink, Christ's apostles pleadingly asked Him, "Master carest thou not that we perish?" (Mark 4:38). No doubt this same question was asked by Mary Ann. Perhaps you too, in the midst of a particularly difficult trial, have wondered if the Lord had abandoned you. Perhaps you too have cried out, "Master, carest thou not?" In each of our lives there will be storms—some with gale-force winds. But the Master's counsel to His disciples is instructive: "Peace, be still." When the time is right, there will come a "great calm" (Mark 4:39)—in our lives and in our troubled hearts.

As time passed, the God of life and love calmed and healed Mary Ann Baker's heart, as He will each of ours. She testified, "The Master's own voice stilled the tempest in my unsanctified heart, and brought it to the calm of a deeper faith and a more perfect trust."[20] Her faith flourished, and like Job of old, she learned things "too wonderful" to know and understand (Job 42:3)—things one can only grasp through the "refiner's fire" (Malachi 3:2).

Desiring to help others whom the Lord had called to pass through the storms and adversities of life, Mary Ann wrote the words of the hymn, "Master the Tempest Is Raging."[21] The lyrics reveal the pain and fear she suffered during her period of darkness. But they also reveal the poignant love and support the Lord offered to her.

Master, the tempest is raging!
The billows are tossing high!
The sky is o'ershadowed with blackness.
No shelter or help is nigh.
Carest thou not that we perish?
How canst thou lie asleep
When each moment so madly is threatening
A grave in the angry deep?

Master, with anguish of spirit
I bow in my grief today.
The depths of my sad heart are troubled.
Oh, waken and save, I pray!
Torrents of sin and of anguish
Sweep o'er my sinking soul,
And I perish! I perish! dear Master.
Oh, hasten and take control!

Note the beautiful, moving chorus as the Lord speaks to us.

The winds and the waves shall obey my will:
Peace, be still. Peace, be still.
Whether the wrath of the storm-tossed sea
Or demons or men or whatever it be,
No waters can swallow the ship where lies
The Master of ocean and earth and skies.
They all shall sweetly obey thy will:
Peace, be still. Peace, be still.
They all shall sweetly obey thy will:
Peace, peace, be still.

Sense the relief and gratitude for the Savior when the storm is calmed in this concluding verse.

Master, the terror is over.
The elements sweetly rest.
Earth's sun in the calm lake is mirrored,
And heaven's within my breast.
Linger, Oh, blessed Redeemer!
Leave me alone no more,

And with joy I shall make the blest harbor
And rest on the blissful shore.

Perhaps Mary Ann Baker was inspired when she penned these words. Without question, she has inspired and helped others through them. She realized her desire and hopes to help others as we pass through difficult times.

Elder D. Todd Christofferson shared an experience where he passed through a rather painful and fearsome storm of life. He bore witness that he and his family learned valuable lessons from the struggle.

Sometime before his call as a General Authority, he had faced a rather significant personal economic challenge—one that had lingered for a number of years. This was not the result of mismanagement or someone's wrongdoing. It was just one of those setbacks that we all face at times in our lives. Nevertheless, the challenge persisted for an extended period—at times worse than others. And it looked as though it might bring about the financial ruin of his family.

Elder Christofferson prayed many times that the Lord would intervene. He pled earnestly for deliverance. But in each case, the answer always seemed to be no. Through the trial, he learned something about his personal prayers. A transition came. He said, "Finally I learned to pray as the Savior did: 'Nevertheless not my will, but thine, be done' (Luke 22:42)."

Elder Christofferson noted that there were times—dark times—when he felt he had nowhere to turn—no other human being that he could call upon for help. Those experiences drove him to his knees, and he found himself in tears begging his Heavenly Father for help. He noted that God always did help. "Sometimes it was nothing more than a sense of peace, a feeling of assurance that things would work out. I might not see how or what the path would be, but He gave me to know that, directly or indirectly, He would open a way. Circumstances might change, a new and helpful idea might come to mind, some unanticipated income or other resource might appear at just the right time. Somehow there was a resolution."

Though it was a period in his life filled with suffering, he noted his gratitude that God did not answer his prayers with some "quick solution" to his seemingly overwhelming problems. The fact that this trial forced him to turn to God for help nearly every day—and for an extended period of time—served as a blessing in his life. He noted that it "taught me truly how to pray and get answers to prayer and taught me in a very practical way to have faith in God. I came to know my Savior and my Heavenly Father in a way and to a degree that might not have happened otherwise or that might have taken me much longer to achieve. I learned that daily bread is a precious commodity. I learned that manna today can be as real as the physical manna of biblical history. I learned to trust in the Lord with all my heart. I learned to walk with Him day by day."[22]

All of us have experienced or will experience raging storms in our lives. They may include financial pressures, a child who has lost their way, a loss of health, some measure of instability, disease, death, relational difficulties, a loss of faith, or myriad other problems. At times these storms can quickly become intense, causing us to suffer deeply. During these trying times, if we seek for an inner peace or stillness amid the chaos, the peaceful reassurance of the Savior will be felt, calmly whispering the words: "Wherefore, be of good cheer, and do not fear, for I the Lord am with you, and will stand by you" (Doctrine and Covenants 68:6). Through the Spirit, we will know that the Lord's promise is true: "For I the Lord thy God will hold thy right hand, saying unto thee, Fear not; I will help thee" (Isaiah 41:13). If the Master can temper the elements, calming the sea, the wind, and waves, He certainly has the power to calm the turbulent times of life as well.

Latter-day Saint composer Michael McLean penned the lyrics to a song that speaks of our desperate need to exercise faith during those inevitable nights of darkness and those periods of adversity. Titled "Hold On," the last verse of the song states:

The message of this moment is so clear;
And as certain as the rising of the sun.
If your world is filled with darkness, doubt, and fear.
Just hold on, hold on, the light will come

The Psalmist declared, "Weeping may endure for a night, but joy cometh in the morning" (Psalm 30:5). Sometimes we feel as though the night will never end, and that we will never feel the warmth and hope the morning sun brings. We might look around and see others seemingly basking in the sun, or experiencing the renewing effects of the morning, and wonder if our long night of darkness will ever end. Yet, if we seek for the Lord's light and love, we *will* find it. It may come in the form of direction, peace, or some other tender mercy. But it *will* come! The Lord has promised us that! Elder Jeffrey R. Holland shared the following encouragement:

> My declaration is that this is precisely what the gospel of Jesus Christ offers us, especially in times of need. There *is* help. There *is* happiness. There really is light at the end of the tunnel. It is the Light of the World, the Bright and Morning Star, the "light that is endless, that can never be darkened." It is the very Son of God Himself. . . . To any who may be struggling to see that light and find that hope, I say: Hold on. Keep trying. God loves you. Things will improve. Christ comes to you in His "more excellent ministry" with a future of "better promises." He is your "high priest of good things to come."[23]

It is inspiring to see those who are able to find the sunshine amid the storms of life; those who are able to follow the Savior's admonition to "be of good cheer" amid daunting difficulties. President Hinckley said,

> Of course there are times of sorrow. Of course there are hours of concern and anxiety. We all worry. But the Lord has told us to lift our hearts and rejoice. I see so many people . . . who seem never to see the sunshine, but who constantly walk with storms under cloudy skies. Cultivate an attitude of happiness. Cultivate a spirit of optimism. Walk with faith, rejoicing in the beauties of nature, in

the goodness of those you love, in the testimony which you carry in your heart concerning things divine.[24]

President Hinckley's counsel here is well summarized by Vivian Greene's famous mantra: "Life's not about waiting for the storm to pass; it's about learning to dance in the rain!"

For those who struggle with "the storms"—who just can't quite muster the faith and trust necessary to optimistically and trustingly traverse what life sends—relationship difficulties are typically the result. Their relationships with God and Christ are strained because they doubt the Father's fidelity to their needs, and they forget Jesus's intimate understanding of what they are personally called to bear (Alma 7:10–13). Thus, they place their trust in their own efforts to "calm the storm," while they neglect to nurture the relationships most capable of aiding them.

Additionally, when we allow ourselves to be overwhelmed by the trials common to all humanity, our relationships with our spouse, children, or other loved ones are strained. Doubt and fear produce stress—and stress strains loving ties and limits our access to the comforting and guiding Spirit of the Lord. "Love at home" is seldom felt and hardly exhibited by those who allow themselves to become consumed by the storm. Healthy relationships with our earthly families require we first have a healthy relationship with our Heavenly family. That can only be accomplished through trust in the Lord Jesus Christ—and that trust is most intensely tested during those occasional "storms."

Our Lord is a "man of sorrows, and acquainted with grief" (Isaiah 53:3). He suffered in every way. He drank the most "bitter cup," and yet He did so without becoming bitter Himself. He "[overcame] the world" (John 16:33). During His most difficult hours, His focus was on others. Indeed, during the time in which He suffered the most, His focus was on each of us. The "Master of oceans, and earth, and skies" loves to bless us; He lives to succor us. He understands us intimately! He has experienced *all* we are going through *and more.* Christ's words to His disciples during Galilee's great tempest can serve as a reminder to us that we need to maintain our faith in Him during turbulent times: "Peace, be still" (Mark 4:39)!

Trials are the means by which we experience growth and development—in our personal lives and in our relationships too. They help us to become the people our Heavenly Father and Jesus Christ want us to be. As we successfully wade through these trials, we are qualified to live with God and Christ again. And in the process, we develop and grow in the strength of our testimonies, our relationships, and our commitment to live the kind of life God would have us live. They are a gift from a good and gracious God who knows better than we do what we truly need.

Quotes to Contemplate:

"I feel like a father with a great family of children around me in a winter storm, and I am looking with calmness, confidence, and patience for the clouds to break and the sun to shine so that I can run out and plant and sow and gather in the corn and wheat and say, Children, come home, winter is approaching again. . . . I am ready to kill the fatted calf and make a joyful feast to all who will come and partake."

—*Brigham Young*

"The Lord God caused that there should be a furious wind blow upon the face of the waters, towards the promised land."

—*Ether 6:5*

"He lives to silence all my fears. He lives to wipe away my tears. He lives to calm my troubled heart. He lives all blessings to impart."

—*"I Know that My Redeemer Lives"*

"It is not without recognition of life's tempests, but fully and directly because of them, that I testify of God's love and the Savior's power to calm the storm."

—*Jeffrey R. Holland*

4

Putting *the* Lord First

"Thou shalt love the Lord thy God with all thy heart, and with all thy soul, and with all thy mind. This is the first and great commandment." —Matthew 22:37–38

AT TIMES WE ALL FEEL AS THOUGH THERE ARE NOT ENOUGH hours in the day to accomplish everything we need to. We've all labored under deadlines, packed schedules, overloaded calendars—having more to do than there is time for. Children, our spouses, our Church callings, our jobs, our houses and yards, and so on—the list of our personal obligations can be mindboggling when we contemplate its breadth. How often have you thought, "If I can just make it through this week, things will settle down!"?

Curiously, with all of the technological advances of our day—things designed to simplify our lives—we seem busier than ever. The microwaves, dishwashers, smart phones, instant messaging, and so on have not slowed things down. They've simply forced us to live lives that are more demanding of our time and attention. With the pace of life seemingly quickening, it is imperative that we not allow the most important thing to be crowded out. Elder Richard G. Scott reminds us, "Make your Eternal Father and His Beloved Son the most important priority in your life—more important than life itself, more important than a beloved companion or children or anyone on earth. Make their will your central desire.

Then all that you need for happiness will come to you."[25] Happiness comes as we keep the Lord's will *first* in our lives, and as we seek to follow His commandments. As the Prophet Joseph taught, "Happiness is the object and design of our existence; and will be the end thereof, if we pursue the path that leads to it; and this path is virtue, uprightness, faithfulness, holiness, and keeping all the commandments of God."[26] There is no other way! (Alma 38:9; Helaman 5:9).

President and Sister Hinckley were wonderful examples of what it means to place and keep the Lord first in your life. Sister Hinckley shared an observation she made early in their marriage:

> As we got closer to marriage, I felt completely confident that Gordon loved me. But I also knew somehow that I would never come first with him. I knew I was going to be second in his life and that the Lord was going to be first and that was okay . . .
>
> It seemed to me that if you understood the gospel and the purpose of our being here, you would want a husband who put the Lord first. I felt secure knowing he was that kind of man. . . . Mother taught us by example that the most wonderful thing in the world was to have a husband who loves the Lord. It did not occur to me that there was any other way to live.[27]

Sister Hinckley supported her husband's desire to keep the Lord first in his life because she knew that if God was first, she would always be a very close second. If Gordon kept the Lord at the center of his life, the Hinckleys' marriage would be what Sister Hinckley wanted it to be. She added, "I knew Gordon was going to devote his life to the Lord. And I couldn't think of anyone I'd rather have him devoted to."[28]

Jesus revealed to Moses the importance of keeping God and Christ as our first priorities. He declared, "And now, Israel, what doth the Lord thy God require of thee, but to fear the Lord thy God, to walk in all his ways, and to love him, and to serve the Lord thy God with all thy heart and with all thy soul" (Deuteronomy 10:12). Luke records for us Jesus's famous interchange with Martha of Bethany. Recall that as the Lord was teaching sacred things to a very attentive Mary, Martha—cumbered with the things of the home—asked Jesus, "Dost thou not care that my sister hath left me to serve alone?" Instructively, the Lord responded, "Martha, Martha, thou art careful and troubled about many things: But one thing is needful: and Mary hath chosen that good part, *which shall not be taken away from her*" (Luke 10:38–42, italics added). The Lord gently reminds His dear disciple that certain things are fleeting and not of eternal import. That which He sought to impart— that which Mary was anxiously receiving—was not fleeting. It would never be taken away. Learning *from* Him and *of* Him was more important than the meal Martha felt an obligation to prepare. While both sisters sought to act in a way that demonstrated that the Lord was important to them, Mary understood that the only food that truly mattered was the spiritual feast Jesus was laying out. Martha, well-meaning as she was, was missing the meal Christ offered her—ultimately putting more importance on the meal she was making than on the meal He was giving. An important lesson was being taught about the need to take time away from the cares of the world so as to make time for the Lord.

Jeffrey R. Holland and his wife Patricia decided early in their relationship to keep the Lord as their first priority. They felt that by keeping the Lord at the center, their relationship would be stronger and the Lord would help them meet and overcome all the demands placed on them. The following experience illustrates their desire to develop the habits that ultimately keep Him first and foremost in one's life:

> Speaking of their early friendship, [Patricia] recalled that when [Jeff] left for his mission, they so wanted to have a "forever kind of love." Together they decided that they would do three things that would unite them even in his absence: (1) Read the scriptures every day. (2) Fast once a week. (3) Pray really often. "These have become habits that we have continued to this day," she said humbly and gratefully, thinking of the far-reaching rewards of that early decision that kept them close while they were far away.

Years passed, and their circumstances were much different from those early days. However, the same principles guided them: daily scripture study, weekly fasting, frequent prayer.

During a particularly busy and difficult stage of their early married life, Brother Holland was a graduate student at Yale University, working on his PhD. Cognizant of the fact that he was one of the few Latter-day Saints students there, he felt the pressure to do well. While working on his doctorate, he was called to serve as a counselor in the stake presidency—a demanding calling that required a considerable amount of time and travel (as the boundaries of their stake were quite large). He was also working as an institute instructor as a means of supplementing their modest income.

At this same time, while trying to mother two small children and maintain a household on a shoestring budget, Sister Holland was called to be the Relief Society president of their ward. "The pressure was so great, I really wanted to give up," she recalled. The three goals they had set seemed so difficult to follow at that stage of their lives. "Read your scriptures more meaningfully," Jeff gently but fervently counseled his young wife. "Because," he said, "the only way we will survive (feeling considerable pressure himself) is through spirituality. We will survive through the strength of the Spirit."

Sister Holland noted how she tried hard to follow that counsel, but she remembered thinking to herself, "That's easier said than done." Nevertheless, being an innately obedient soul, she was determined to try. Seeking to apply her husband's counsel, as hard as it was, she fasted and prayed on one of those difficult days. "His words kept coming to my mind about reading the scriptures more meaningfully. I remember walking over to my scriptures with the attitude, okay, we'll just see if there's something to this. And of course there was. The answers were there."[29]

In Doctrine and Covenants 101:16, the Lord counsels us, "Therefore, let your hearts be comforted concerning Zion for *all flesh* is in mine hands; be still and know that I am God" (italics added). "All flesh" implies *everything*! All of our lives, the lives of our children, our work, our Church assignments, our relationships, our financial issues, our trials, etcetera! The Lord truly has all things in His hands. We should live as though we believe that, and as though we find comfort in that reality!

Of course, it is important to take the time to be "still." When we are busy, rushing from project to project, we may miss those promptings that inevitably come to those who seek to place the Lord first in their lives. President David O. McKay shared the following story of a tragedy that befell a member of the Presiding Bishopric.

> One day in Salt Lake City a son kissed his mother good morning, took his dinner bucket, and went to City Creek Canyon where he worked. He was a switchman on the train that was carrying logs out of the canyon. Before noon his body was brought back lifeless. The mother was inconsolable. She could not be reconciled to that tragedy—her boy just in his early twenties so suddenly taken away. The funeral was held, and words of consolation were spoken, but she was not consoled. She couldn't understand it. One forenoon, so she says, after her husband had gone to his office to attend to his duties as a member of the Presiding Bishopric, she lay in a relaxed state on the bed, still yearning and praying for some consolation. She said that her son appeared and said, "Mother, you needn't worry. That was merely an accident. I gave the signal to the engineer to move on, and as the train started, I jumped for the handle of the freight car, and my foot got caught in a sagebrush, and I fell under the wheel. I went to Father soon after that, but he was so busy in the office [i.e., his Church calling] I couldn't influence him—I couldn't make any impression upon him, and I tried again. Today I come to you to give you that comfort and tell you that I am happy."[30]

Imagine being so busy in one's Church calling that you're not receptive to the influence of the Holy Ghost. Taking the time to be still is paramount to having the Lord at the center of your life. It means slowing down and daily taking the time to pray, study truth, ponder its meaning and application, and seek to create an environment wherein one can readily feel the Spirit. The hymn "Be Still, My Soul" reminds us that as we create a "stillness" in our lives, we can come to know "the Lord is on our side." If we wish to have heavenly guidance active in our life, we must follow the example of Mary rather than that of Martha in this story. This applies to callings as well as the mundane things of life. Having "down time," "quiet time," or "sacred time" alone not only shows our Eternal

Father that He is the most important priority in our lives, but it also allows us to "know that He is God" and to feel His strength and influence. And with that strength and influence we can meet the demands that are ours.

President Henry B. Eyring taught, "There is another way to look at the problem of crowded time. You can see it as an opportunity to test your faith." He continued:

> The Lord loves you and watches over you. He is all-powerful, and He promised you this: "But seek ye first the kingdom of God, and his righteousness; and all these things shall be added unto you" (Matthew 6:33). That is a true promise. When we put God's purposes first, He will give us miracles. If we pray to know what He would have us do next, He will multiply the effects of what we do in such a way that time seems to be expanded. He may do it in different ways for each individual, but I know from long experience that He is faithful to His word.

Concluding this thought, President Eyring stated, "He will answer your prayer and He will keep His promise to add upon your head blessings, enough and to spare. Those apparent prison walls of 'not enough time' will begin to recede, even as you are called to do more."[31]

In our years of Church service, one of the things we have learned is that the families that have the fewest problems—the families who struggle least when they have trials—are those who put the Lord first. Ironically, those who question how much the Church "asks" of its members—those who complain that the Church requires *too much* time and money, and takes mom or dad or the kids out of the home *too* frequently—are *not* the ones with the most successful and well-adjusted families. More often than not, it is those who place the Lord first—those whose children know whom Mom and Dad serve—that fare the best in life, trials, relationships, and so on. None of us bless our families by placing God second or third. When we do, the natural result is a family raised on Sunday outings that replace church. And a generation later, we find ourselves wondering why our kids are inactive when we spent so much time with them in their youth. If parents place God first, their children will most likely learn to do the same. If, on the other hand, parents place Him second or third in their lives, their kids will—at best—place the Lord a distant fourth or fifth.

The Great Exemplar, Jesus Christ, demonstrated that He kept the "first and great commandment" by spending time drawing closer to the Father through meditation, pondering, and prayer. "Then was Jesus led up of the Spirit into the wilderness to be with God" (Joseph Smith Translation, Matthew 4:1 [in Matthew 4:1, footnote b]). The Savior's main desire was to "do always those things that please[d]" His Father (John 8:29). The example He set for us in trials is also noteworthy. Jesus's experience in Gethsemane is certainly a testament to His love for us. But it is also a profound witness of how committed He was to the Father's will and way. His willingness to endure the unfathomable that the Father might have His will met is an invitation to each of us to follow His example, even in our trials. And as we center our lives on God and Christ, the ultimate outcome will be our ability to gracefully endure all that we're called to traverse, thereby leading us to an eternal inheritance in their presence.

Quotes to Contemplate

"When we put God first, all other things fall into their proper place or drop out of our lives."

—*Ezra Taft Benson*

"Thou shalt have no other gods before me."

—*Exodus 20:3*

"The only things we can keep are the things we freely give to God. What we try to keep for ourselves is just what we are sure to lose."

—*C. S. Lewis*

"Most men [and women] do not set priorities to guide them in allocating their time, and most men forget that the first priority should be to maintain their own spiritual and physical strength. Then comes their family, then the Church, and then their professions—and all need time."

—*Harold B. Lee*

"Serve [the Lord] with all your heart, might, mind and strength."

—*Doctrine and Covenants 4:2*

5

Learning *to* Laugh *at* What Life Throws Your Way

"God hath made me to laugh." —Genesis 21:6

THESE ARE INTERESTING TIMES WITH CHALLENGES UNLIKE anything the world has experienced in any previous age. In addition to temptations that seem ever mounting, the rush, stress, and constant noise of our day make the achievement of the ideal family seem like a distant and unlikely goal. With all we have on our plates in these very busy times—work, school, extracurricular activities, church and community service, and so forth—many feel overwhelmed and stressed by the reality that their plate is constantly full of things that just *must* be done! The familiar refrain "Where can I turn for peace?" may be vocalized more often on our knees in desperation than it is on a pew in adulation. As a consequence, many of us are prone to feel stressed and unhappy, when we should be feeling the exact opposite—living in this, the greatest dispensation in the history of the world.

One reason so many of us struggle with feelings of discontent, stress, and unhappiness is our natural tendency to take life just a bit more seriously than we should. Our inability to laugh at ourselves and our circumstances has hindered our ability to have the very joy God designed mortality to have (2 Nephi 2:25). The proverb reminds us, "A merry heart doeth good like a medicine" (Proverbs 17:22). Elder Joseph B. Wirthlin indicated that their family made it a practice to substitute laughter for anger. That had a healing and enlivening influence for them. He told of one occasion when the family was headed south from Salt Lake to Cedar City. They took a wrong turn but were unaware of it for two hours, until they saw the sign stating, "Welcome to Nevada." Rather than becoming angry, they simply laughed and created what he described as a "cherished memory." Elder Wirthlin taught by example the importance of looking for humor in potentially frustrating situations.

> I remember when one of our daughters went on a blind date. She was all dressed up and waiting for her date to arrive when the door-bell rang. In walked a man who seemed a little old, but she tried to be polite. She introduced him to me and my wife and the other chil-dren; then she put on her coat and went out the door. We watched as she got into the car, but the car didn't move. Eventually our daughter got out of the car and, red faced, ran back into the house. The man that she thought was her blind date had actually come to pick up another of our daughters who had agreed to be a babysitter for him and his wife.
>
> We all had a good laugh over that. In fact, we couldn't stop laughing. Later, when our daughter's real blind date showed up, I couldn't come out to meet him because I was still in the kitchen laughing. Now, I realize that our daughter could have felt humili-ated and embarrassed. But she laughed with us, and as a result, we still laugh about it today. [32]

This example from Elder Wirthlin's life offers a valuable anti-dote to the stress, frustration, disappointments, and embarrassments of mortality. When trials or disappointments come—and they *will* come!—you have a choice to make. You can either laugh or cry; feel frustrated or faith-filled! But, ultimately, the choice is yours—and the God-given power to decide is within each of us. Hartley Coleridge wrote, "And laughter oft is but an art, to drown the outcry of the heart."[33] Laughter can be exactly that—our way of responding to situations that make us want to cry—or scream! Elder Wirthlin sug-gested, "The next time you're tempted to groan, you might try to laugh instead. It will extend your life and make the lives of all those around you more enjoyable."[34] President Gordon B. Hinckley suggested that we not simply learn to replace frustrations with joviality, but that we actually become the type of people who see the world with a positive perspective. He counseled, "We need to have a little humor in our lives. We better take seriously that which should be taken seriously, but at the same time we can bring in a touch of humor now and again. If the time ever comes when we can't smile at ourselves, it will be a sad time."[35] Being able to laugh at our foibles and failings is evidence that we have the Spirit of the Lord with us. As President Heber C. Kimball noted, "I am perfectly satisfied that my Father and my God is a cheerful, pleasant, lively, and good-natured Being. Why? Because I am cheerful, pleasant, lively, and good-natured when I have His Spirit."[36] The Lord has promised to aid those who seek to see humor in the difficult circumstances of life. To Job, who had incomprehensibly difficult trials, we find this promise: "Behold, God will . . . fill thy mouth with laughing, and thy lips with rejoicing" (Job 8:20–21). To His disciples Jesus promised "Blessed are ye that weep now: for ye shall laugh" (Luke 6:21).

If we seek to find humor and happiness in the trying experiences of life, we will be healthier and happier; more energetic and more loved. And, ultimately, we will be more functional tools in the hands of the Lord.

Quotes to Contemplate

"To everything there is a season, and a time to every purpose under the heaven: . . . A time . . . to laugh; . . . and a time to dance."

—*Ecclesiastes 3:14*

"The only way to get through life is to laugh your way through it. You either have to laugh or cry. I prefer to laugh. Crying gives me a headache."

—*Marjorie Pay Hinckley*

"The true believer is serious about the living of his life, but he is of good cheer. His humor is the humor of hope."

—*Neal A. Maxwell*

"Man is distinguished from all other creatures by the faculty of laughter."

—*Joseph Addison*

6

Never Seek *to* Change, Control, *or* Criticize

"When we undertake to . . . exercise control or dominion or
compulsion upon the souls of the children of men, in any degree
of unrighteousness, behold, the heavens withdraw themselves; the
Spirit of the Lord is grieved." —Doctrine and Covenants 121:37

A T THE CONCLUSION OF EACH OF THEIR WEEKLY MEETINGS, the members of the Canadian *Possum Lodge* huddle as they offer the famous "Man's Prayer," which states: "I'm a man, but I can change, if I have to, I guess." While we lightheartedly make fun of the dramatic differences that exist between most men and women, it is quite a serious reality that not a few marriages suffer from contentions and frustrations over a spouse who seems unwilling to change or conform to the wishes and likes of his or her mate. Somehow we forget the eternal verity: "He that complies against his will, is of his own opinion still."[37] Forced conformity seldom makes a convert to the opinions of a husband or wife. Indeed, the spouse who seeks to force a partner to change or submit to his or her thinking ultimately fights a losing battle, and likely does much to destroy the most sacred of all relationships.

In Asia, there is a profound principle for living life known as *wu-wei* (pronounced "woo-way"). The term means quite literally "inaction"—but, by implication, it denotes one should not fight against the experiences life sends your way. To do so is to harm yourself because you miss the opportunities for growth inherent in the day-to-day struggles of life. Among other things, *wu-wei* teaches us that we should never seek to better or change others. People are the way they are for a reason. You're welcome and encouraged to change yourself, but you should not seek to change others. As one text notes, "Conscious efforts to control people and events are counterproductive."[38] The spouse that is constantly controlled, criticized, or forced to change and conform most likely will come to resent the controlling partner. A colleague of ours shared an experience that illustrates the danger of insisting that a spouse be what *we* want him or her to be:

> A group of sisters—in a "newly wed/nearly dead" ward in Utah— had gathered for their quarterly enrichment meeting. As the evening developed a couple of the sisters, who had only been married a few short years, began to grouse about how annoying their husbands are—and about all of the things they do wrong seemingly every hour of the day!
>
> One noted: "My husband constantly leaves his socks on the floor. I'm sick and tired of picking up after him. If he continues to do it, I swear, I'm going to strangle him!" The young sister to whom she was speaking concurred, and shared that her husband was also "annoying beyond belief!"
>
> Sitting in the back of the room were two faithful sisters, each widowed nearly two decades. Overhearing the conversation, and the frustrations of many of the younger married sisters, the widow of eighteen years said to the widow of twenty years: "Oh, how I wish I had socks on my floor!"

Curiously, what was to one a curse "annoying beyond belief" was to another a gift—a blessing! One sister was filled with loathing for her husband because of a definite weakness that he had, while another would gladly "put up with" all such weaknesses, just to enjoy the gift of God, which is eternal companionship. From the example of these good Latter-day Saint sisters we learn that efforts to change others often provoke the antithesis of happiness and, in many cases, fill us with disappointment, disenchantment, and ingratitude. They are damaging to relationships and damaging to our spirits. Indeed, when we seek to change others rather than changing ourselves, we typically find ourselves filled with frustration or bitterness, and we certainly don't become more Christlike in the process. When we fight to clone the world after our own images and views, the Spirit of the Lord is not operative in our lives, and the joy and diversity, which make this life beautiful and palatable, are certainly lost.

President Gordon B. Hinckley once noted, "Unfortunately, some women want to remake their husbands after their own designs. Some husbands regard it as their prerogative to compel their wives to fit their standards of what they think to be the ideal. It never works."[39] Heavens! Almost without exception, the thing that attracted us to our mates was not that they were the same as us but, rather, that they were significantly different! But then, once married, we seem bent on removing the very thing that drew us to our partner in the first place! What a contradiction we are as humans.

After observing President Monson's treatment of Sister Monson, Elder Neil L. Anderson of the Twelve pointed out, "He has never asked Sister Monson to be anyone different than she is."[40] Similarly, Sister Marjorie Pay Hinckley wrote, "Gordon always let me do my own thing. He never insisted that I do anything his way, or any way, for that matter. From the very beginning he gave me space and let me fly."[41] She added: "Early on I realized it would be better if we worked harder at getting accustomed to one another than constantly trying to change each other—which I discovered was impossible. Try not to be too demanding of one another. There must be a little give and take, and a great deal of flexibility, to make a happy home."[42] Elder Marion D. Hanks of the Seventy wisely defined a good marriage as follows:

> Friendship in a marriage is so important. It blows away the chaff and takes the kernel, rejoices in the uniqueness of the other, listens patiently, gives generously, forgives freely. Friendship will motivate one to cross the room one day and say, "I'm sorry; I didn't mean that." It will not pretend perfection nor demand it. It will not insist that both respond exactly the same in every thought and feeling,

but it will bring to the union honesty, integrity. There will be repentance and forgiveness in every marriage—every good marriage—and respect and trust.[43]

A spouse who is a true friend never seeks to change, control, or criticize his or her partner. Rather, such a spouse looks for the best and forgives freely the worst!

As painful as it may be to hear, those who seek to change their spouse—rather than love them for who they are—are selfish! And if they do not focus on changing themselves they will find they are in an unhappy and unfulfilling relationship—one largely of their own making. The gospel teaches us that this life is about growth and change—but not the growth and change of others. As we seek to overcome feelings of resentment toward a partner and his or her annoying idiosyncrasies, the Lord will bless us to not only love our spouse more deeply, but also to no longer be bothered by his or her uniqueness. The happiness and contentment that will follow are incalculable.

One might summarize the counsel of the prophets and apostles with the following point: "Do what Jesus would do!" And what would He do? He would serve those who hate Him and act inconsiderately toward Him. He would love the unlovable. He would look past petty faults—which are often the ones *we* find the most annoying! He would do all in His power to show love, forgiveness, understanding, compassion, and helpfulness—and in that process He would find Himself filled with the Spirit of God. President Gordon B. Hinckley taught, "I have long felt that the greatest factor in a happy marriage is an anxious concern for the comfort and well-being of one's companion. In most cases selfishness is the leading factor that causes argument, separation, divorce, and broken hearts."[44] We must follow the Lord's example and the prophet's counsel. If we wish to be happy, and wish to be deeply in love with our husband or wife, this is how we must live. As we lay down our lives in the service of our spouse, God will change us into what He is and will cause us to be filled with love for those we serve! What a glorious gift for our token acts of sacrifice!

Quotes to Contemplate

"The secret of a happy marriage is to serve God and each other. . . . Paradoxically, the more we serve one another, the greater is our spiritual and emotional growth."

—*Ezra Taft Benson*

"The most important relationship upon this earth for you is between you and your sweetheart. Work at it, sacrifice for it, enjoy it."

—*George I. Cannon*

"We kill with our hard opinions."

—*William Shakespeare*

"The man [or woman] who never alters his [or her] opinion is like standing water, and breeds reptiles of the mind."

—*William Blake*

7

True Love & Friendship *within* Marriage

*"Many waters cannot quench love, neither can the
floods drown it." —Song of Solomon 8:7*

ＩN GREEK, THERE ARE FOUR WORDS THAT MIGHT RIGHTLY BE
translated as "love" in English. *Agape* is typically understood to
mean a "godly" or "godlike love." It is the love God feels for us
and the love that we, as faithful Christians, *should* feel for others.[45]
Phileo usually implies "love between friends"—hence Philadelphia
is the "city of brotherly love." *Eros* is associated with the "physical love between a man and his wife"—though it was traditionally
understood to go beyond just physical love. There was usually a
strong emotional, even spiritual, side to *eros*.[46] And finally, *Epithumia* was, quite simply, a "lust" for that which is forbidden.

We live in a world today that speaks much of "love." Romance
novels fly off the shelves, and movies about love (a.k.a. "chick flicks")
are often box-office smashes. However, our use of the word seems
highly distorted, and the contemporary fixation is certainly more on
"lust" than actual "love." Indeed, if one analyzes media portrayals
of "love," I would venture to guess that nine times out of ten what
the movies or novels refer to as "love" is really *epithumia* or unbridled "lust." This seems to be the case, even when what's depicted
is supposed to be the typical relationship between a husband and

wife. We are bombarded daily with images, lyrics, and portrayals of what society calls "love," but which are really nothing of the kind. It is no wonder that so many today are addicted to pornography. It is not only readily available, but we are constantly confronted with the equivalent of pornographic images in the advertisements we see, the entertainment available to us, and even in the clothing of many we encounter. The rising generation has lived their entire lives in a society that consciously and corruptly calls *lust* "love"!

Unquestionably, love between a husband and wife—that which God would have us feel, express, and experience—has a physical component to it. This aspect of the marital relationship has been declared sacred by living prophets and apostles. It is a gift from God! It is important, is sanctioned, and should bring a power to the bond between a man and woman that nothing else can. But there is an emotional side of marital intimacy that is also important—that melding of the minds and wills of two people that quite literally fulfills the Lord's injunction: "Be one, even as [I and my Father] are one" (John 17:22). In *no* relationship does this exist at the beginning—and for most it takes many, many years to fully develop. But the key to its accomplishment is conscious work. As Elder Jeffrey R. Holland noted, "Second only to your membership in the Church, your 'membership in a marriage' is the most important association you will have in time and eternity—and to the faithful what doesn't come in time *will* come in eternity."[47] But we must be willing to work to nurture and develop that celestial status so many of us dream about *prior* to marriage, and that so many of us *after* marriage fret for. As we've noted elsewhere in this little work, President Hinckley taught, "True love is not so much a matter of romance as it is a matter of anxious concern for the well-being of one's companion."[48] And Elder Holland noted, "You know, winning Sister Holland was not an easy thing to do. I worked at it and worked at it and worked at it."[49] Elder Russell M. Nelson shared an experience he had with his wife, Dantzel, which is a testament both to their "true love and friendship" for each other, and also to how one develops such:

Her love for me motivated her to teach school during the early years of our marriage. When things were tight, she held a second job at night. Once when things were exceptionally tight, she even sold her blood in between her two jobs to keep us solvent. (Her dear parents may have wondered what kind of a son-in-law they had on that occasion!) I thought of that many years later when she needed a transfusion urgently and her blood couldn't be matched readily with donor blood from the blood bank. What a privilege it was for me to donate mine directly to her. [50]

Sacrifice, service, giving, forgiving, and thoughtfully attending to the needs *and wants* of one's partner is the surest way to fall deeply in love with our chosen mate. The Victorian poet Elizabeth Barrett Browning penned the oft-quoted refrain, "How do I love thee? Let me count the ways?" Commenting on the profundity of her words, Elder Holland shared this: "I am impressed with her choice of adverb—not *when* do I love thee nor *where* do I love thee nor *why* do I love thee nor *why don't* you love me, but, rather, *how*. *How* do I demonstrate it, *how* do I reveal my true love for you? Mrs. Browning was correct. Real love is best shown in the 'how.'"[51] Setting aside situations of abuse, those most dissatisfied with their marriage are those who want *their* needs to be met, but do a minimal amount to meet the needs of their partner. Jesus taught, "It is more blessed to give than to receive" (Acts 20:35). If we wish to receive, we must give to our partner. We must place his or her needs and desires above and before our own. To borrow a line from Truman G. Madsen, we "somehow, someday, must reach the point at which we hold our physical life cheap . . . even to the point of being willing to lay our life down in the image and pattern of the Lord Jesus Christ."[52] Our Savior willingly and constantly gave of Himself to bless those whom He served. He forgot His own needs and wants and met those of others. In so doing, He didn't feel empty and deprived, but filled—filled with divine love. As you and I follow the counsel of President Hinckley, developing an "anxious concern" for the well-being of our spouse, the Lord will bless us that we will *not* feel deprived, but be filled with love—and in so doing, we will draw the love and friendship

43

of our companion to us. It is paradoxical but right: true love blossoms when we care more about our spouse than we care about ourselves. When we get to that point, all of our needs and wants *will* be met. That is the promise of the Lord!

Now perhaps a word or two about friendship is in order. Marital partners begin as friends. And yet tragically, too many *end* their friendship when they *begin* their marriage! Among Latter-day Saints, such should never be the case. However, with the hustle and bustle of day-to-day living—getting an education, raising a family, earning an income, serving in the Church, maintaining a household, and running children from event to event—too many place their marriage on the back burner! Everything seems to get nurtured *except* the friendship that, prior to marriage, we did everything in our power to cultivate. Husbands and wives *must* place their marriage before *any other* earthly relationship or temporal thing. Ultimately, it must come before their relationship with other family members, before work, before leisure activities, before a calling; it must be second only to one's relationship with God. The neglected plant dies. And the neglected friendship does too. Successful couples who are also successful friends (1) date regularly, (2) seek to develop interest in each other's favorite things, (3) look for activities that they can find mutual enjoyment in, (4) make time to chat about their day, their work, their children, their concerns, their joys, and their accomplishments—to chat about each other!

True love and true friendship *can be* ours—but each can be achieved *only* upon the principles discussed above. The spouse who says, "Fine, when my husband/wife begins doing these things, I will too!" shall never experience the joy of true love. However, the one who decides today "This I will do, from this day forward!" will surely discover a love and friendship beyond anything imagined.

Quotes to Contemplate

"Knowing that we should love is not enough. But when [that] knowledge is applied through service, love can secure for us the blessings of heaven."

—*David B. Haight*

"Love is a lack of personal selfishness."

—*Theodore M. Burton*

"Love seeketh not itself to please, Nor for itself hath any care. But for another gives its ease, And builds a Heaven in Hell's despair."

—*William Blake*

"A faithful friend is the medicine of life."

—*Ecclesiasticus 6:16*

"Love is only chatter, Friends are all that matter."

—*Gelett Burgess*

8

Christlike Communication

"How forcible are right words." —Job 6:25

UNFORTUNATELY, A COMMON COMPONENT IN THE AGING process is often hearing loss. Hearing aids can sometimes help but seldom restore the wearer to full auditory strength. President Marion G. Romney shared the following experience regarding his wife's apparent hearing loss:

> I once went to see a doctor about her hearing. He asked me how bad it was, and I said I didn't know. He told me to go home and find out. The doctor instructed me to go into a far room and speak to her. Then I should move nearer and nearer until she does hear. Following the doctor's instructions, I spoke to her from the bedroom while she was in the kitchen—no answer. I moved nearer and spoke again—no answer. So I went right up to the door of the kitchen and said, "Ida, can you hear me?" She responded, "What is it, Marion— I've answered you three times."[53]

As humorous as the experience sounds, losing one's hearing and, thus, not being able to communicate is a terribly frustrating experience. Perhaps even more frustrating is the experience of talking to a friend or employer who does not suffer from hearing loss, but who doesn't seem to be willing to listen to (or hear) something you're trying to convey. Most couples have had the unpleasant experience of talking with their spouse, but feeling as though he or she simply doesn't "get it" or isn't listening. The wedge this drives between partners is deep and dangerous. We laugh about John Gray's book title *Men are from Mars, Women are from Venus*, but some couples find this is more truth than fiction when it comes to their attempts to communicate with each other. Unfortunately, because of communication struggles, some reach the point where they treat strangers better than those they love. If men and women do not consciously focus on developing good communication skills with their spouse, it is quite possible to lose one's "listening ear" and see the communication in the relationship deteriorate. Though a dramatic example, the famous "Seven Ages of the Married Cold" highlights this process of communication deterioration.

> **Year 1** — "Honey, I'm really worried about you. You've got a bad sniffle and there's no telling about these things with all the strep going around. You jump in bed and I'll take care of everything."

> **Year 2** — "Listen, darling, I don't like the sound of that cough. I've called Doc Miller and I'm off to get a prescription. I think you ought to relax a little. The house looks fine."

> **Year 3** — "Maybe you better lie down, sweetheart. Nothing like a little rest when you feel lousy. After the dishes are finished, I think you ought to hit the sack, don't you?"

> **Year 4** — "Look, dear, be sensible. Take a couple of aspirin. There is no need to try to clean the whole house when you aren't feeling well. It'll still be here tomorrow."

> **Year 5** — "Good grief, why don't you take a couple of [lozenges]? You sound terrible!"

> **Year 6** — "For Pete's sake, stop sneezing! You are going to give us all pneumonia!"

> **Year 7** — "If you'd just gargle or something instead of sitting around barking like a seal, I'd appreciate it."[54]

If things can get this bad by year seven, imagine a marriage of thirty, forty, or fifty years. Heavens, imagine a marriage for eternity with someone who does not communicate! (Of course, without good communication, no marriage is eternal.)

As would be expected, the Savior set the perfect example in how we could communicate with others. There are a number of principles of communication that we can learn from Him. First of all, the words He used to communicate had a positive impact on those with whom He interacted. His motive was ever to lift, build, and support those around Him. There were times when He spoke plainly to His disciples to help them understand and to grow. However, He always did so in a spirit of love and encouragement. Additionally, there were times when Jesus had to chasten and correct people so that they could progress in the development of divine attributes. Again, His motive was their blessing and betterment. Jesus spoke according to His hearer's needs. Thus, we often find Him speaking mercifully, lovingly, and kindly to individuals whose lives were not as they should be, such as the woman taken in adultery. As we become like Him, we also use our words to build and strengthen people and to express our love for others.

Like Jesus, the Father is depicted in scripture as being exemplary in how He speaks to those of His family—those whom He loves. For example, He refers to Jesus as His "Beloved Son." On another occasion, the Father added His personal appreciation for Jesus by saying, "This is my Beloved Son, in whom I am well pleased." Like the Father, Jesus throughout scripture models how to express love to other people (Doctrine and Covenants 124:15). Christ spoke kindly about people when He was with them, and when He was not. His words were not simply wise, but also comforting and supporting. As we become like Him, our communication reflects His. In 1 Corinthians 2:16, the Apostle Paul speaks of the faithful followers of Jesus as developing the "mind of Christ." Elder Bruce R. McConkie noted when we "walk in the light as he is in the light . . . [we] thereby have his mind. [We then] think what he thinks, know what he knows, *say what he would say*, and do what he would do . . . all by revelation from the Spirit."[55] Those who have sought to develop the "mind of Christ" speak gently and listen intently when someone needs to be heard. They take the time to listen when their interest, support, and love are important to the person who seeks their ear, their thoughts, their heart, and their empathy. Those who have the "mind of Christ" have developed His way of communicating, so that they (through their words) can help and bless others, just as Jesus (through His words) helped and blessed others.

A story from the life of Elder Russell M. Nelson illustrates the need to follow the Spirit, and, in so doing, to say the right words at the right time.

The early days of open-heart surgery were unchartered territory. Consequently, misfortunes often occurred—one of which Elder Nelson would never forget.

Prior to the advent of cardiac surgery, a young couple Dr. Nelson encountered had lost a child to a congenital heart defect. When he operated on their second child, who also had heart problems, the surgery was unsuccessful and the child died. A few years later, this same couple came to Dr. Nelson with a third infant, also suffering from a heart ailment. Filled with hope and trusting in his abilities, they brought their baby to him for treatment of its malformed heart. Despite his best efforts, this child too died shortly after the operation. In sorrow, Elder Nelson noted that in his grief he felt inconsolable.

Arriving home from work on the day the third child had died, he told the story to his wife, and in tears exclaimed, "I'm through. I'll never do another heart operation as long as I live!" Dr. Nelson cried most of the night. The dark hours preceding dawn were largely spent kneeling beside a chair in the living room. All he could think of were those parents who had lost three children—and how all of his medical training could not provide them with the blessing they so desperately desired.

"Words cannot describe my feelings of pain, despair, grief, and tragedy," he said. "These characterizations only scratch the surface of the torment raging in my soul, which caused me to determine that my failures and inadequacies would never be inflicted on another human family."

Sister Nelson had also spent a sleepless night worrying—praying. As the sun rose that morning, she told her grief-stricken husband, "If you quit now, someone else will have to learn all over again what you know. Isn't it better to keep trying than to quit now and require others to go through the same grief of learning what you already know?"

Dr. Nelson saw the wisdom in what his wife was telling him. He determined to work a little harder, to learn a little more, and to strive even harder for perfection in his field. That morning he returned to his lab to "chart the uncharted sea."[56]

Sister Nelson's words to her husband during this difficult trial were clothed in love, compassion, and understanding. The effect of her words helped him to not give up but, rather, to continue in his practice. Her Spirit-directed words ultimately blessed countless individuals whose lives were saved by his continued practice of medicine. She was not only gentle in what she spoke, but she was also inspired. Christlike communication is not just the sharing of words; it is the wise sharing of feelings, emotions, and concerns—all in a spirit of love and affection. As the Nelsons have taught us by their example, our words can have a profound impact on others.

The scriptures warn us not to use our words to injure each other. In the Epistle of James we are instructed, "If any man among you seem to be religious, and bridleth not his tongue, but deceiveth his own heart, this man's religion is vain" (James 1:26). James goes on to warn us about the unbridled tongue and the damage it can do:

> Even so the tongue is a little member, and boasteth great things. Behold, how great a matter a little fire kindleth! And the tongue is a fire, a world of iniquity: so is the tongue among our members, that it defileth the whole body, and setteth on fire the course of nature; and it is set on fire of hell. For every kind of beasts, and of birds, and of serpents, and of things in the sea, is tamed, and hath been tamed of mankind: But the tongue can no man tame; it is an unruly evil, full of deadly poison. (James 3:5–8)

In a letter to the Colossians, the Apostle Paul wrote, "Put off all these; anger, wrath, malice, blasphemy, filthy communication out of your mouth" (Colossians 3:8). Similarly, James counseled, "Let every man be swift to hear, slow to speak, slow to wrath: For the wrath of man worketh not the righteousness of God" (James 1:19–20). Words clothed in anger, pride, or selfishness can dampen relationships, and they certainly chase away the Lord's Spirit. The old adage is true: relationships must be treated like bank accounts. If each day we make withdrawals, but we never make an equal number of deposits, it will not take long before we have depleted our account. Christlike communication is made up of daily deposits of kindness, love, and understanding. These are crucial if a marriage is to stay out of the red. Be wise and accumulate as many credits as possible.

Though none of us are perfect in our communications, those who hope to have a content marriage and a happy home must strive to become more like Jesus in the way they live and in the way they speak. As with all things, Christ is our exemplar—including in how we should communicate with others. He was ever encouraging and strengthening to others, and as we reach out to Him, He will ever help us in our journey to develop His attributes—including the ability to "speak with the tongue of angels" (2 Nephi 31:13).

Quotes to Contemplate

"Cease to find fault one with another."

—Doctrine and Covenants 88:124

"For in many things we offend all. If any man offend not in word, the same is a perfect man, and able also to bridle the whole body."

—James 3:2

"For our words will condemn us."

—Alma 12:14

"We must be prudent and discreet and yet be willing to communicate, for true brotherhood is such that our friends and families will blow away the chaff in our communications—and do so with the breath of kindness."

—Neal A. Maxwell

"I have learned that the head does not hear anything until the heart has listened, and that what the heart knows today the head will understand tomorrow."

—Jones Stephenson

9

Making Family *a* Priority

"Take especial care of your family from this time, henceforth
and forever." —Doctrine and Covenants 126:3

THOSE WHO SERVE IN LEADERSHIP RESPONSIBILITIES WITHIN
the Church are often overwhelmed at the time required to
faithfully serve the Lord and to adequately bless His children. And yet, the sacrifices we make as local leaders are nothing
when compared to that of the Brethren. They and their spouses are
among the busiest people in the world. Because so much of their
time is spent building the kingdom, and because they hold callings that quite literally consume their lives, they must consciously
ensure that they make time for their families. Drawing upon his
own experience as a busy priesthood leader, President Dieter F.
Uchtdorf taught: "The wise . . . resist the temptation to get caught
up in the frantic rush of everyday life. They follow the advice 'There
is more to life than increasing its speed.' In short, they focus on the
things that matter most." He then added, "In family relationships
love is really spelled *t-i-m-e*, time."[57]

President Thomas S. Monson learned the importance of priori-
tizing and placing first things first when he and Sister Monson had
their first child. His biographer explained:

> [S]ince Frances and the baby would be staying in the hospital for more than a week, as was the custom then, Tom went ahead with a fishing trip in Idaho that he had planned. He says he has never heard the end of it. His story is that Frances encouraged him to go, promising she would "just rest" till he was back. Frances has "mentioned" the expedition and its timing "many times."' He is a "serious" fisherman. But that fishing trip was a "serious" mistake.[58]

As much as President Monson loves fishing and hunting, there can be no doubt that he never placed sport above spouse again. Notwithstanding the "serious" mistake, he has always valued his family time and has desired to make lasting memories with his children and grandchildren.

One of his granddaughters wrote what it is like having President Monson as her grandfather. "As I've grown, I've realized that President Monson is, indeed, a wonderful best friend to have." One of his great gifts, his granddaughter pointed out, is his love for creating memories. President Monson is an "activity planner" when it comes to his family. He loves to have fun. "We loved our fishing outings, going to breakfast, and trips to the amusement park. I distinctly remember thinking that my Grandpa was very cool because he rode with me on the roller coaster at Lagoon and on Space Mountain at Disneyland!"

If by definition a "best friend" is someone who takes a sincere interest in your life, then President Monson qualifies. We are all familiar with stories of how the Spirit has prompted him to show an interest in one of Heavenly Father's children. His one-on-one care for others is an example to all of ministering as the Lord would minister. However, President Monson's care and concern for members of the Church is simply an outgrowth of how he is as a father, grandfather, and great-grandfather. His granddaughter continues: "It was always a nice feeling to know that Grandpa was proud of my good grades, and he always attended my piano recitals. He was also interested in my friends. When I was dating my husband, Grandpa called and asked us out on a 'double date' to the symphony. I thought nothing of it as I was accustomed to spending a lot of time with my grandparents. My husband, however, later confessed that he had never been more nervous for a date in his life!"[59]

President Monson offered the following caution about the use of time: "We become so caught up in the busyness of our lives. Were we to step back, however, and take a good look at what we're doing, we may find that we have immersed ourselves in the 'thick of thin things.' In other words, too often we spend most of our time taking care of the things that do not really matter much at all in the grand scheme of things, neglecting those more important causes."[60] There will always be demands, deadlines, and pressures in our day-to-day lives. This is particularly true of those with young families or new careers—as it is for those serving in positions of responsibility in the Church. However, as we listen with our hearts we will hear frequent reminders from Heaven to slow down, to enjoy people, and to share moments that are meaningful with them. Education, employment, Church meetings, personal interests, and so on, are all important, but family relationships are eternal—they are one of the few things the Lord has commanded that we make a priority in our lives.

Elder Dallin H. Oaks highlighted the fact that not all "good" choices in life are of equal worth. There are many commendable actions that are not the "best" choice, even though they are acceptable choices. Yet it is the nature of most human beings to misprioritize, occasionally placing "good things" before the "best things."[61] Elder Oaks said, "I have never known of a man who looked back on his working life and said, 'I just didn't spend enough time with my job.'"[62] Spending quality and quantity time with children is one of the *best* ways we can use our sacred and limited time. Being there to listen; to understand what they are experiencing; to reassure them when they are discouraged; and to support them when they face trials or rejection, or experience shattered dreams—these are the things that matter most. A ball game on TV, pursuing a promotion at work, or spending time on a hobby are all moral and respectable pursuits. But they must *never* come before our sacred responsibilities to spouse and children. The "best" use of our time *necessarily* places our families above our professional or personal interests. What single worldly accomplishment could ever hold a candle to drying the tear of a son or daughter—or shedding a tear with them? What personal accolades are more worthy of celebrating above the accomplishments of a child or grandchild? Encouraging and comforting; praising and teaching; playing and praying—these are the things of which memories are made. There is so much good we can do—good of an eternal nature—when we look beyond ourselves and toward those who God has entrusted to our care.

Elder Richard G. Scott stressed the importance of spending quality time with children and grandchildren. He noted an important lesson he had learned from his wife. His job required extensive travel. On one occasion, he had been gone from home for almost two weeks straight. When he arrived home on Saturday morning, he learned that their washing machine was on the fritz, and that his wife had been doing the laundry by hand in the bath tub. He had a Church meeting in four hours but, having an engineering background, he was convinced that he could fix it in the time available.

His wife, Jeanene, saw him tearing apart the machine and asked, "Rich, what are you doing?" He replied, "I'm repairing the washing machine so you don't have to do this by hand." She said to him, "No. Go play with the children." To which he responded, "I can play with them anytime. I want to help you." Sister Scott said in a recognizable tone, "Richard, please go play with the children." Elder Scott noted that whenever his wife spoke to him "authoritatively," he "saluted and obeyed."

He shifted gears and went outside to his children. They rolled around in the fall leaves. They chased each other around the house. They had a marvelous time. A few hours later he went to his Church meeting. Elder Scott noted, "I probably would have forgotten that experience." However, what happened a matter of hours later helped him to internalize the importance of what had just taken place with his children. "The next morning, about 4:00 a.m., I was awakened as I felt two little arms around my neck, a kiss on the cheek, and these words whispered in my ear, which I will never forget: 'Dad, I love you. You are my best, best friend.'" In sharing this experience, Elder Scott asked, "Are you having that kind of experience with your children? If you are not, you are missing one of the supernal joys of life. If you have not yet married, you can decide now that when you are a parent the happiness of your children will be a very high priority in your life."[63]

As we all know, time passes by too quickly—and for parents it won't be long until busy homes, once filled with children's voices and laughter, become all too quiet, devoid of such beautiful, cheerful, even heavenly noise. It doesn't seem to take long for playrooms, including all their clutter, to be emptied and changed into neat and tidy rooms absent of the little angels that once marked those cherished moments. Yet, with time passing by so quickly, it is imperative we create lasting memories with our loved ones. In speaking on using our time wisely, Elder Neal A. Maxwell counseled us to use our agency "in such a way that we do the things that matter most, so that these things [or people] are not at the mercy of the things that matter least."[64] As we learn to prioritize our time, may we remember to not allow "good" things to crowd out the essential things in life. It has been said, "The key is not to prioritize what is on your schedule, but to schedule your priorities."[65]

Quotes to Contemplate

"The property which we inherit from our Heavenly Father is our time, and the power to choose in the disposition of the same. This is the real capital that is bequeathed unto us by our Heavenly Father."
—*Brigham Young*

"It's not enough to be busy; so are the ants. The question is, what are we busy about?"
—*Henry David Thoreau*

"Lost time is never found again. You may delay, but time will not."
—*Benjamin Franklin*

"Time is the most valuable thing a man can spend."
—*Theophrastus*

10

Avoiding *the* Enticements *&* Entanglements *of the* World

"Know ye not that the friendship of the world is enmity with God? Whosoever therefore will be a friend of the world is the enemy of God." —James 4:4

I**N THE ENTIRE HISTORY OF THE WORLD, THIS IS PERHAPS THE** most amazing and glorious time to be alive. The comforts and conveniences that are available to us are unparalleled. The standard of living many of us enjoy would be the envy of any of our ancestors. Even our ability to spread the gospel has been enhanced by the amazing advancements in technology and travel. What a gift God has given us by allowing us to dwell at this time, with all of its attendant blessings and opportunities.

Though many of us have been richly blessed, and the Church has prospered significantly, too many who profess faith in the restored gospel are also enticed by the things of this world and, in harkening to those enticements, find themselves "entangled . . . in the vanities of the world" (Doctrine and Covenants 20:5). Satan lies to us that temporal things are important, and that appearances matter. True, we must feed, clothe, and shelter ourselves. But we would do well to follow the counsel of Paul: "And having food and raiment let us be therewith content" (1 Timothy 6:8; see also Philippians 4:11). There is certainly nothing evil about temporal blessings.

However, they become "evil" when we don't simple *use* them in life; but we let them *into* our lives. As a poet wrote:

> All the water in the world, no matter how it tried
> Could never sink the smallest ship, unless it got inside.
> All the evil of the world, and every kind of sin
> Could never damn a human soul, unless we let it in.[66]

The things of this world become "evil" when we become addicted to them, or when they corrupt our thinking about ourselves, others, or what truly matters in life. We certainly have the power to control worldliness and the role it plays in our personal lives. However, if we "let it in," we may rest assured that it will then control us! Elder Marvin J. Ashton taught,

> If our top priorities are constantly directed toward the acquisition of more and better worldly goods, it will not take long to increase our love in those directions. The purchase of a larger house or a nicer car or a more expensive boat may cause us to sacrifice our resources and develop an unwise love for these symbols of success and pleasure. We learn to love that which we serve, and we serve that which we love.[67]

Similarly, President Ezra Taft Benson noted: "Christ taught that we should be in the world but not of it. Yet there are some in our midst who are not so much concerned about taking the gospel into the world as they are about bringing worldliness into the gospel."[68] Conscious efforts to straddle the line between Babylon and Zion are counterproductive. Some of us are guilty of trying to live in both worlds. "Even if we decide to leave Babylon, some of us endeavor to keep a second residence there, or we commute on weekends."[69] Such an approach will not allow us to have the Spirit of the Lord actively in our lives.

Of course, Christ is our exemplar. And the world was appalling to Him. Similarly, there are many stories from the lives of the prophets and apostles of this dispensation that attest that they too reject the standards, philosophy, and trappings of this fallen world.

For example, when President Boyd K. Packer was dating Donna

Smith, whom he later married, he had arranged to take her to a high school dance. Unfortunately, the only family vehicle available to him that evening was his father's "home-made wrecker." It was an old, heavy-duty touring car that had been chopped and welded into a one-seater monstrosity with a heavy back-frame and a hand-crank. President Packer described it as "pure ugly." No doubt he was hesitant to take a girl he wished to impress, dressed in her best clothing, for a ride in such an eyesore. However, he thought this might be a good test as to whether she was a potential marriage partner. "If she'll ride with me in this," he thought, "we can go through life with few problems." When he arrived to pick Donna up, she "took his arm and stepped into the wrecker as unconcerned as if it were up to the standard that Boyd desired for her." He noted that her "lack of concern about riding with him in the old wrecker" impressed him. This was no worldly gal! It also "gave him confidence" when they decided to marry "to negotiate with a local realtor on the purchase of an old, run-down home in the southeast part of the city. It had been owned by a bachelor who had recently died. The home captured Boyd's interest as a place that he and Donna could restore and beautify. It was financially feasible and would be well within a teacher's income."[70] What a grand litmus test of a potential spouse. As the early years of *nearly every* marriage are financially lean, a lack of worldly attachment is ever so important. Donna Smith was unattached to the world; and young Boyd snatched her up!

Of course, the entrapments of worldliness are not to be avoided *only* in the early, financially poor years of a marriage. Many, having been married a number of years and having achieved a decent income have, nevertheless, become so entangled in worldly enticements that they are in debt up to their eyeballs! The strain debt causes on a marriage and family—to say nothing of what it does to the Spirit in one's life—is almost unbearable. We must recognize the temptation to engross ourselves deeply in the things of this world for what it is—a temptation of the adversary. He wants us to be in bondage. He wants to strain our relationships. He wants us to be so busy slaving to pay our debts that we cannot serve in the kingdom.

He wants us to see things and people through worldly lenses so that we will make choices that will harm ourselves, our families, and others around us. A great story from the lives of President and Sister Hinckley comes to mind. One of their daughters records:

> Mother was getting ready for an occasion when I dropped by the apartment late one afternoon. When she told me where she was going—as she reached for her pleated skirt and white cotton blouse—I gasped. "Mother, this is a huge thing," I protested. "The reception is in honor of Dad and you. He's probably going to wear a tux. Every woman there will have on sequins and diamonds." Continuing to dress, completely unruffled, she said, "Well, I don't have any sequins in my closet. But this skirt is black, and the blouse does have a lace collar. And besides that, if we're the guests of honor, whatever I wear will have to be right!"[71]

Sister Hinckley taught an important principle. People are to be loved for who they are, not for what they wear or own. One of the great lies of Satan, by which he seeks to entice and entrap us, is that "what you see is what you get!" This is often false in products we buy, and it is *never* true in human beings. We do ourselves and others a grave injustice when we judge on appearances, possessions, education, occupation, experience, etcetera. This is how the world judges. It is how Satan would have us judge. God makes no such judgments before He extends His love to us. Therefore, we must not make these types of critical, unfair, and uninformed judgments when we seek to learn about and love others.

Another example, highlighting the dangers of worldliness and materialism, comes from the life of a friend of mine. Happily married in the temple, he and his wife set out to raise a family and serve in the Church while he gained his education and then began a rather successful career in a potentially lucrative field. He worked hard, and he was blessed. He succeeded professionally and, consequently, reaped significant monetary blessings. However, the reward of his labors was more than his wife could handle. Status and "things" became the hallmark of her life. Her husband's desire to serve in the Church was an inconvenience she initially tolerated but eventually rejected. This gifted, compassionate, and faithful brother—a man with tremendous gifts as a leader—found himself in a position twenty years earlier he would have thought impossible. The sweetheart of his youth now wanted her Sundays back, her tithing back, and a lifestyle inconsistent with a temple-going, Church-loving Latter-day Saint. The choice she insisted he make was the gospel or her. Unexpectedly, he found himself divorced; and all of the worldly success turned from being a blessing to being a curse. As is well known, money is one of the leading causes of divorce. Of course, it is not the money that causes the problems. It is succumbing to the enticements of the world. We are reminded of Paul's oft-misquoted instructions to Timothy. The Apostle did *not* say, "money is the root of all evil" but, rather, that "the *love of* money is the root of all evil" (1 Timothy 6:10, italics added). It is the addiction to—the corruption by—the things of this world that the Lord warns us of. And a fixation on worldly achievements or success will *ever* cause problems in families and relationships.

As wonderful as "things" are, we must be careful that they are not the most important "things" in our lives. Worldliness—in the form of money, looks, possessions—is enticing. But it is also addictive and binding. It can enslave us intellectually, temporally, spiritually, and even morally. The Lord has warned us time and again about the dangers of worldliness: "Take heed to yourselves, lest at any time your hearts be overcharged with . . . [the] cares of this life" (Luke 21:34). "For what is a man profited, if he shall gain the whole world, and lose his own soul?" (Matthew 16:26).

> No man can serve two masters: for either he will hate the one, and love the other; or else he will hold to the one, and despise the other. Ye cannot serve God and mammon. Therefore I say unto you, Take no thought for your life, what ye shall eat, or what ye shall drink; nor yet for your body, what ye shall put on. Is not the life more than meat, and the body than raiment? Behold the fowls of the air: for they sow not, neither do they reap, nor gather into barns; yet your heavenly Father feedeth them. Are ye not much better than they? . . . And why take ye thought for raiment? Consider

the lilies of the field, how they grow; they toil not, neither do they spin: And yet I say unto you, . . . if God so clothe the grass of the field, . . . shall he not much more clothe you, O ye of little faith? Therefore take no thought, saying, What shall we eat? or, What shall we drink? or, Wherewithal shall we be clothed? . . . for your heavenly Father knoweth that ye have need of all these things. But seek ye first the kingdom of God, and his righteousness; and all these things shall be added unto you. Take therefore no thought for the morrow: for the morrow shall take thought for the things of itself. (Matthew 6:24–34)

President Spencer W. Kimball lamented:

Many people spend most of their time working in the service of a self-image that includes sufficient money, stocks, bonds, investment portfolios, property, credit cards, furnishings, automobiles, and the like to guarantee carnal security throughout, it is hoped, a long and happy life. Forgotten is the fact that our assignment is to use these many resources in our families and quorums to build up the kingdom of God—to further the missionary effort and the genealogical and temple work; to raise our children up as fruitful servants unto the Lord; to bless others in every way, that they may also be fruitful. Instead, we expend these blessings on our own desires, and as Moroni said, "Ye adorn yourselves with that which hath no life, and yet suffer the hungry, and the needy, and the naked, and the sick and the afflicted to pass by you, and notice them not" (Mormon 8:39).

As the Lord himself said in our day, "They seek not the Lord to establish his righteousness, but every man walketh in his own way, and after the image of his own God, whose image is in the likeness of the world, and whose substance is that of an idol, which waxeth old and shall perish in Babylon, even Babylon the great, which shall fall." (Doctrine and Covenants 1:16)[72]

Faithful Saints should regularly evaluate the degree to which the world has crept into their lives and hearts. Elder Dallin H. Oaks pointed out: "Materialism, which gives priority to material needs and objects, is obviously the opposite of spirituality."[73] To what degree do you place the things of God (that is, callings, service, offerings, and people) first in your life? Whose kingdom do you seek to build first: your own, or God's? Is there *anything* you place before the Lord and your family? President James E. Faust once noted, "No stone wall separates the members of the Church from all of the seductions of the world. Members of the Church, like everyone else, are being surfeited with deceptions, challenges, and temptations. However, to those of enduring faith, judgment, and discernment, there is an invisible wall which they choose never to breach."[74]

Quotes to Contemplate

"The cares of the world are so many and so entangling, even very good people are diverted from following the truth because they care too much for the things of the world."

—*Spencer W. Kimball*

"I would rather walk barefoot from here to the celestial kingdom . . . than to let the things of this world keep me out."

—*N. Eldon Tanner*

"This is my scripture: They who long and lust after the fashions of the world are destitute of the Spirit of God."

—*Brigham Young*

"We have been warned against the things of this world . . . But exactly what are the things of the world? An easy and infallible test has been given us in the well-known maxim 'You can have anything in this world for money.' If a thing is of this world, you can have it for money; if you cannot have it for money, it does not belong to this world."

—*Hugh Nibley*

"And again I would exhort you that ye would come unto Christ, and lay hold upon every good gift, and touch not the evil gift, nor the unclean thing."

—*Moroni 10:30*

11

The Importance *of* Temples *&* Covenants

"Serve him day and night in his temple." —Revelation 7:15

A NUMBER OF YEARS AGO, AFTER HAVING SPENT THE EVE-ning in the Oakland Temple, I (Alonzo) exited to find that the sun had set, and the city of San Francisco—visible from the temple across the bay—was illuminated, creating a postcard perfect scene. The Oakland Temple has a balcony on the roof that allows patrons to stand on top of the Lord's house and look out over the bay and into the city of San Francisco. That night, though by the world's standards it was beautiful, as I looked upon the famous "city by the bay" I was struck with how perfectly it symbolized this fallen world, with all of its vices and enticements. Having spent the last few hours in the temple, rather than being drawn to this visually stimulating picture, I felt to retreat back into that place of holiness—that refuge from the world!

In December 1832, the Lord commanded the Saints to "organize yourselves; prepare every needful thing; and establish a house, even a house of prayer, a house of fasting, a house of faith, a house of learning, a house of glory, a house of order, a house of God" (Doctrine and Covenants 88:119). To the Quorum of the Twelve as they prepared to serve missions, the Prophet Joseph said, "You need an endowment, brethren, in order that you may be prepared and able to overcome all things."[75] In introducing the notion of a temple to the Saints at Kirtland, Ohio, the Lord indicated that it was a place for holy habits: a place to pray, fast, and learn. It was a place where order would reign, and where order could be found—but also a place where the glory of God *could* be present and manifest to those prepared to receive it.

Why temples? Why, in this dispensation, did the Lord indicate that such were necessary? What is the power and purpose of those covenants? Three salient truths must be noted.

First, in the house of the Lord—via the sealing keys that have been restored through the instrumentality of the Prophet Joseph Smith—families can be bound together for all eternity. Elder Richard G. Scott shared a personal experience relating to this principle.

His wife was pregnant with their third child. At that same time, their second child was seriously ill. When the doctors performed their fluoroscopic examinations of the young boy, Sister Scott would hold him on her lap—unaware that she was being exposed to excessive amounts of radiation. Consequently, the child within her womb died, and she was unable to have further children. The heartache the Scotts felt was incalculable. Yet, Elder Scott noted, we *do* have these children—we have them for eternity. Why? Because they were born in the covenant, and that is the blessing of participating in the ordinances of the holy temple. Families who have been sealed in the temple, and who seek to keep their covenants, have the promise of the Lord that they will be together forever! Elder Scott testified:

> I know that I will have the privilege of being with that beautiful wife, whom I love with all my heart, and with those children who are with her on the other side of the veil, because of the opportunities made possible through the eternal ordinances that were performed in the . . . temple. What a blessing to have once again on the earth the sealing authority, effective not only for this mortal life but for the eternities. I am grateful that the Lord has restored His gospel in its fullness, including the ordinances that are required for

us to be happy in the world and to live everlastingly joyous lives in the hereafter.[76]

One of the most important reasons for the temple, and its sacred covenants, is its ability to unite families, not only for time, but also for all eternity! For those who have learned to love as Christ loves, what a blessing and promise this offers!

A second reason the Lord has restored temple ordinances in this dispensation is for the salvation of the dead. In Section 188 of the Doctrine and Covenants, the Lord declared that the "salvation" of our dead "is necessary and essential to our salvation, as Paul says concerning the fathers—that they without us cannot be made perfect—neither can we without our dead be made perfect" (Doctrine and Covenants 128:15). The vast majority of the world has lived either in a time when the fulness of the gospel—and its exalting ordinances and covenants—were not upon the earth, or in a location wherein they did not have access to these same salvific gifts. Thus, we must work for their salvation by performing these ordinances, and entering into these covenants, on their behalf. Most will be familiar with the time the signers of the Declaration of Independence appeared to President Wilford Woodruff, who "urged him to help redeem them by doing their temple work";[77] evidencing the reality that the dead desire these ordinances and need them for their salvation. Of course, Section 128 reminds us that we cannot "be made perfect" without doing these works on their behalf. This is true, partially because we are accountable (by covenant) to do these sacred things for those who cannot do them for themselves. But also because the temple affects us as we so do—which leads us to our next point.

Though not tertiary in significance, a third reason for the restoration of temple ordinances and covenants are their direct effect upon the soul who engages in them. Were these rites solely for the dead, I suspect the Lord could shorten what is required of *us* to redeem *them*. I've always assumed that the narrative of the Creation and Fall could be told, or acted out, just as readily on the other side of the veil as they are here. However, you and I as fallen mortals *need* to engage in those rites for our dead because, in so doing, we change ourselves. As we regularly go through the temple, the temple goes through us. We become sanctified. We become changed. We begin to see things as they really are. (cf. Jacob 4:13). We become more like our Father in Heaven and our Savior, Jesus Christ. President Ezra Taft Benson noted, "Our attendance there blesses the dead and also blesses us."[78] President Gordon B. Hinckley stated, "I am satisfied that every man or woman who goes to the temple in a spirit of sincerity and faith leaves the house of the Lord a better man or woman. There is need for constant improvement in all of our lives. There is need occasionally to leave the noise and the tumult of the world and step within the walls of a sacred house of God, there to feel His spirit in an environment of holiness and peace."[79] Again, from Elder Scott:

> Since my dear wife was called home, I have kept a personal commitment to participate in some way in temple ordinances each week. I will continue to do so. When travel on assignment has precluded temple attendance, upon return I have attended more frequently to maintain my commitment. I do not have the capacity to express meaningfully the enduring peace and serenity and the inexpressible joy that have come from that temple worship . . . Come to the temple, now. It will greatly bless your life.[80]

While different from Elder Scott's experience, nevertheless illustrative of a similar principle, we find the following curious story from the life of Elder Marriner W. Merrill of the Quorum of the Twelve. Elder Merrill had been serving as president of the Logan Temple when he learned of the power of the temple and the adversary's awareness of how it poses a threat to his work. President Rudger Clawson, of the First Presidency, recounts the experience:

> A rather large entourage of strange looking souls appeared on the grounds of the temple, and their spokesman approached Elder Merrill. The Apostle said to him: "Who are you and who are these people who have come up and taken possession of the temple

unannounced?" The uninvited visitor answered: "I am Satan and these are my people. . . . I don't like the work that is going on in this temple and feel that it should be discontinued. . . . I will tell you what I propose to do . . . I will take my followers, and will instruct them to whisper in the ears of the people, persuading them not to go to the Temple, and thus bring about a cessation of your Temple work." Satan then withdrew. [81]

President Merrill, commenting on this strange interview with the evil one, said that for quite a period of time the spirit of indifference to temple work seemed to take possession of the people and very few came to the house of the Lord. Satan, who is the enemy of all righteousness, is clearly displeased with temple work and its potential influence upon our lives.

During a recent visit to the home of a member of my stake, I (Alonzo) noticed that this family—whom I did not really know— had pictures on their walls of two newborns. I inquired and learned that both had been born prematurely and then died. The parents, completely inactive, had never been sealed in the temple. Prominently displayed in their living room were pictures of Christ, the temple, and the famed declaration "Families Are Forever." A bit confused by the seeming contradiction, but urged on by the unmistakable prompting of the Spirit, I asked this couple who were (at this point) but acquaintances: "Do you not want these two precious children to be yours for eternity? Why are the two of you not getting yourselves prepared to enter the temple and be sealed as a family?" This same question could be asked of any of us, not just those who have lost children, or who have failed to be sealed in the temple. Those of us who do not attend the temple regularly negate all three purposes of the house of the Lord: eternal families, redeemed ancestors, and personal perfection—and we do so at the peril of our own salvation. Ask yourself these questions: "Do I not wish to be with my family forever? If the temple is not part of my life, can I honestly expect that I will reap the blessings of the Lord's house? How, aside from attending the temple regularly, do I expect the Lord to perfect me, save my deceased ancestors, and keep (or put) in place the sealing between husband and wife—parents and children?" If the temple is not part of my life now, my family will not be part of my life for eternity.

An Apostle of the Lord Jesus Christ has born witness of the power and peace that come from frequent and regular temple attendance. Another member of the Twelve has warned of how desperately Satan wishes to keep us from the holy temple. With prophetic utterances such as these—and in a world filled with so many trials and troubles—who among us can afford to go without this blessing, strength, and protection? We need to attend the temple regularly because it will give us strength against temptation, patience in affliction, context for that which we encounter, and love for the Lord and His work! Such attributes will not be developed on their own—and few, if any of us, can foster them without that additional help found in the Lord's holy house.

Quotes to Contemplate

"As we strive to keep our temple covenants and build strong marriages and families, we fortify ourselves with a shield of faith to protect us from the fiery darts of the adversary."

—*Robert D. Hales*

"How far is heaven? It is not very far: in the temples of God, it is right where you are."

—*Thomas S. Monson*

"Our temples are testaments of our faith in the everlasting family."

—*James E. Faust*

"When we . . . leave the cares of the world outside, wonderful things happen which cannot be described. The Spirit of the Lord distills upon one's soul in these holy houses. . . . A new perception comes into focus of who we are, of what this life is really about, of the opportunities of eternal life, and of our relationship with the Savior."

—*Victor L. Brown*

"A temple is a retreat from the vicissitudes of life."

—*Franklin D. Richards*

12

Becoming One

"I say unto you, be one; and if ye are not one ye are not mine" —Doctrine and Covenants 38:27

IN 1971 THE U.S. SUPREME COURT RULED UNANIMOUSLY THAT "forced busing" of students was permissible in order to achieve racial desegregation. In accordance with that decision, that same year the city of Alexandria, Virginia, decided to integrate its school system. As part of that transition, T. C. Williams High School appointed a new head football coach—an African American man by the name of Herman Boone. The difficulties Coach Boone faced in his attempts to meld an all-white high school football team with one that was all-black were beyond anything that could have been imagined. Through persistence and a great deal of opposition, however, the racially mixed team came together—forgetting their differences in deference to their common goal. In the coach's pep talk prior to their first game, he reminded them: "Tonight we've got Hayfield. Like all the other schools in this conference, they're all white. They don't have to worry about race. We do. Let me tell you something: you don't let *anyone* come between us. *Nothing* tears us apart." T. C. Williams High School went on to win the 1971 Virginia State Football Championship. Their struggle to develop unity changed not only their season, but also their lives.[82] Coach Boone's words apply as much to marriages as they do to football teams. A stable marital relationship is one in which spouses strive to not let *anything* come between them, nor to allow *anything* to tear them apart!

Modern-day prophets and apostles exemplify what it means to be "one" with your spouse. One such example is President Gordon B. Hinckley, who described his marriage to Marjorie as follows:

> May I be personal for a moment? I sat across the table from my wife the other evening. It was fifty-five years ago that we were married in the Salt Lake Temple. The wondrous aura of young womanhood was upon her. She was beautiful, and I was bewitched. Now, for more than half a century, we have walked together through much of storm as well as sunshine. Today neither of us stands as tall as we once did. As I looked at her across the table, I noted a few wrinkles in her face and hands. But are they less beautiful than before? No, in fact, they are more so. Those wrinkles have a beauty of their own, and inherent in their very presence is something that speaks reassuringly of strength and integrity and a love that runs more deeply and quietly than ever before.[83]

On another occasion, President Hinckley, reflecting on his marriage, said: "[Ours] has been a happy and wonderful and rewarding marriage. We have known lean times and fat times, bad times and good times. We have loved and respected one another. There is cause for much of gratitude and gladness."[84] The Hinckleys found happiness together because they were headed the same direction. They had become one, and thus the natural "pulls" and "tugs" of the mortal experience didn't "pull" and "tug" at their marriage. They were "equally yoked," and thus equally happy!

As couples walk through life together, striving to become one, they must necessarily abandon their selfishness and pride along the path to perfection. If they are to become one, they must truly believe that neither one is more important than the other. As Elder Marion D. Hanks noted, "Men and women are of equal value before God and must be equally valuable in the eyes of each other."[85] It has become somewhat of a colloquialism to say of Adam and Eve that she was "not made out of his head to rule over him, nor out of his feet to be trampled on by him, but out of his side to be equal with him, under his arm to be protected, and near his heart to be beloved."[86] Oneness in a relationship comes less from *giving in to* your spouse, and more from loving the Lord. As two partners individually and collectively submit themselves to Christ, they find little to divide them. They will naturally support, sustain, and serve each other. And, in the process of time, they will find that they have grown together as one, because they have learned to love and serve the One—their good and gracious God.

Elder Bruce R. McConkie taught "the Creation, the Fall, and the Atonement are the three pillars of eternity."[87] Similarly, most marriages have their "three pillars"—a creation, a fall, and an atonement. The "creation" is the beginning of the relationship—the honeymoon stage where everything seems blissful, new, and exciting. But inevitably most marriages experience a "fall"—trials, adversity, challenges, and even fits of disenchantment. It isn't just sinful couples that go through this stage. Many of the Brethren have spoken candidly about the difficult times in their lives and relationships. Brigham Young, for example, had a wife who left the Church. The marriage of Joseph F. Smith to his first wife ended in a bitter divorce. Spencer W. Kimball and his wife had their occasional disagreements—one of the most famous being when Sister Kimball wanted to save their extra cash for a new house. Spencer, on the other hand, wanted to take the money and travel. They could not come to an agreement, so Camilla and the children stayed home while Spencer loaded up the car and went on a family vacation, by himself.[88] Of his relationship with his wife, Elder Dallin H. Oaks once shared this: "Our children can't claim that they've never heard us disagree. . . . June and I have had some *marvelous* disagreements."[89] Many of us will have difficulties in our relationships. Thankfully, the Atonement of Jesus Christ can heal all wounds, and it can provide us with the strength to endure those inevitable challenges. When a husband and wife utilize Christ's gifts, and thereby become *like* Him because they live committed *to* Him, then the atonement stage of the marriage is realized. Their trials are less devastating, their love is more mature, and their unity is assured. They begin to see fewer flaws in their spouse, they are more forgiving of weaknesses, they are less prone to frustration, and the joy of the journey becomes surprisingly grand.

One additional insight into a man and woman's achievement of "oneness" can be drawn from the story of the Fall. We are told that Adam and Eve were "naked," and yet "not ashamed" (Genesis 2:25; Moses 3:25; Abraham 5:19). Nakedness is sometimes a symbol for being innocent or right with God. Scripture informs us that when we are righteous our "confidence [will] wax strong in the presence of God" (Doctrine and Covenants 121:45). We feel no fear of judgment or condemnation because we have lived honest and true to covenants, to God, and, in the case of a marriage, to our spouse. The "nakedness" of Adam and Eve reminds us as husbands and wives to be transparent and completely honest with our spouse. There can be no hidden addiction, no inappropriate conversations with members of the opposite sex, and no unfaithfulness physically or even emotionally. If a marriage is to be eternal, there must be absolute fidelity—and that requires absolute openness, transparency, and honesty. The surge of pornography and social media romances in our day are inexcusable for those who would be "one" with their spouse. Where mistakes have been made, the Atonement can bring forgiveness to the transgressor and healing to the wounded spouse. However, unless a companionship achieves the openness described, that marriage will not be on the path to eternity.

Although the Father and Son are separate and distinct beings, they are perfectly united in purpose and scope. As couples become one, they each retain their own identity, their own personality, but (like the Father and Son) they become one in unity, purpose, love, and scope. As Jesus said, "If ye are not one ye are not mine" (Doctrine and Covenants 38:27). The key to achieving oneness with our eternal partner is to be found in achieving oneness with our God. Through that process we will acquire their attributes, their vision, and we will act in harmony with their will. Then, and only then, will we be enabled to *live happily ever after*!

Quotes to Contemplate

"Unity is power."

—*Joseph Smith*

"They were of one heart and one mind."

—*Moses 7:18*

"Marriage, in its truest sense, is a partnership of equals."

—*Gordon B. Hinckley*

"Marriage is . . . the union of two souls in a strong love for the abolishment of separateness. . . . It is the golden ring in a chain whose beginning is a glance, and whose ending is Eternity."

—*Kahlil Gibran*

"Be ye not unequally yoked together."

—*2 Corinthians 6:14*

Notes

1   Brian Kolodiejchuk, editor, *Mother Teresa: Where There is Love, There is God (New York: Image, 2010), 288.*

2   John Donne, "Meditation XVII," cited in *The Oxford Dictionary of Quotations,* third edition (New York: Oxford University Press, 1980), 190.

3   Robert D. Hales, "President Henry B. Eyring: Called of God," *Ensign*, July 2008, 11–13.

4   *Teachings of Presidents of the Church—Harold B. Lee* (Salt Lake City, UT: Intellectual Reserve Incorporated, 2000), 182–83; David O. McKay, *Gospel Ideals* (Salt Lake City, UT: Bookcraft, 1998), 525–26.

5   Richard L. Evans, "A Reaffirmation: 'We Thank Thee O God for a Prophet,'" Conference Report, October 1958, 60.

6   Richard L. Evans, "One Small Step," *Improvement Era*, June 1970, 38.

7   Jeffrey R. Holland, "How Do I Love Thee?," *Brigham Young University 1999–2000 Speeches, 5–6.*

8   See James P. Bell, *In the Strength of the Lord: The Life and Teachings of James E. Faust* (Salt Lake City: Deseret Book, 1999), 194.

9   James E. Faust, "The Value of Self-Esteem," address given at a CES Fireside for Young Adults, May 6, 2007, Salt Lake Tabernacle.

10   Bell, 144.

11   Bell, 218.

12   Robert D. Hales, "Seek and Attain the Spiritual High Ground in Life," *CES Fireside for Young Adults*, March 1, 2009, Brigham Young University.

13   "Master, the Tempest Is Raging," *Hymns of The Church of Jesus Christ of Latter-Day Saints* (Salt Lake City, UT: The Church of Jesus Christ of Latter-day Saints, 1985), 105.

14   Spencer W. Kimball, *The Teachings of Spencer W. Kimball*, Edward L. Kimball, editor (Salt lake City, UT: Bookcraft, 1998), 252.

15   Jeffrey R. Holland, "How Do I Love Thee?," 5.

16   Bruce R. McConkie, *Doctrinal New Testament Commentary*, three volumes (Salt Lake City, UT: Bookcraft, 1987–1988), 3:302.

17   Robert D. Hales, "Seek and Attain."

18   Jeffrey R. Holland "How Do I Love Thee?," 5.

19   Ernest K. Emurian, *Living Stories of Famous Hymns* (Boston, MA: W. A Widdle, 1955), 83–85.

20   "Our Latter-Day Hymns," quoted in Phil Kerr, *Music in Evangelism* (Glendale, CA: Gospel Music Publishers, 1939), 167–69.

21   "Master the Tempest is Raging," *Hymns*, 105.

22   D. Todd Christofferson, "Give Us This Day Our Daily Bread" in *CES Fireside for Young Adults*, January 9, 2011, Brigham Young University.

23   Jeffrey R. Holland, "An High Priest of Good Things to Come," Conference Report, October 1999, 45.

24   Gordon B. Hinckley, "If Thou Art Faithful," *Ensign*, November 1984, 92.

25   Richard G. Scott, "The Power of Correct Principles," *Ensign*, May 1993, 34.

26   Joseph Smith, *Teachings of the Prophet Joseph Smith*, Joseph Fielding Smith, compiler (Salt Lake City, UT: Deseret Book, 1976), 255.

27   Sheri L. Dew, *Go Forward with Faith* (Salt Lake City, UT: Deseret Book, 1996), 114–15.

28   Marjorie Pay Hinckley, *Glimpses into the Life of Marjorie Pay Hinckley*, Virginia H. Pearce, editor (Salt Lake City, UT: Deseret Book, 1999), xi.

29   See Ardeth G. Kapp, "'The Only Way to Be Happy': Pat Holland," in *New Era*, April 1981, 40.

30   David O. McKay, *Gospel Ideals* (Salt Lake City, UT: Bookcraft, 1998), 525–26.

31   Henry B. Eyring, "Education for Real Life," *Ensign*, October 2002, 14.

32   Joseph B. Wirthlin, "Come What May and Love It," *Ensign*, November, 2008, 26–27.

33   Hartley Coleridge, "Address to Certain Gold-fishes," Henry Davidoff, editor, *The Pocket Book of Quotations* (New York: Pocket Books, 1952), 180.

34   Joseph B. Wirthlin, "Come What May and Love It," 27.

35   Gordon B. Hinckley, "Excerpts from Recent Address of President Gordon B. Hinckley," *Ensign*, October 1996, 73.

36   Heber C. Kimball, in *Journal of Discourses*, 4:222.

37   Samuel Butler, *Hudibras,* cited in *The Pocket Book of Quotations* (New York: Pocket Books, 1952), 256.

38   Brandon Toropov and Father Luke Buckles, *The Complete Idiot's Guide to World Religions*, third edition (Indianapolis, IN: Alpha Books, 2004), 244.

39   Dew, *Go Forward With Faith, 166.*

40   Neil L. Anderson, "Interview with Neil L. Andersen, 7 October 2008," cited in Heidi S. Swinton, *To the Rescue: The Biography of Thomas S. Monson* (Salt Lake City, UT: Deseret Book, 2010), 510.

41   Marjorie Pay Hinckley, *Glimpses into the Life of Marjorie Pay Hinckley*, Virginia H. Pearce, editor (Salt Lake City, UT: Deseret Book, 1999), 190.

42   Hinckley, Glimpses, 184.

43   Marion D. Hanks, "Eternal Marriage," *Ensign*, November 1984, 36–37.

44   Gordon B. Hinckley, *Discourses of President Gordon B. Hinckley, two volumes* (Salt Lake City, UT: The Church of Jesus Christ of Latter-day Saints, 2004–2005), 2:214.

45   Agape is a love that, for humans, is born out of veneration or esteem, which we should feel for God and Christ. Phileo, on the other hand, comes from emotion. Christ commands us to have Agape, but never commands us to have Phileo, "because love as an emotion cannot be commanded, but only love as a choice." See James H. Thayer, *Thayer's Greek-English Lexicon of the New Testament* (Peabody, MA: Hendrickson Publishers, 1999), 653. See also 3–4.

46   The ancient Greeks sometimes used the term *Eros* to describe the ecstasy of communing with God through a spiritual experience.

47   Jeffrey R. Holland, "How Do I Love Thee?," 2.

48 Gordon B. Hinckley, "Except the Lord Build the House . . . ," *Ensign*, June 1971, 71.

49 Holland (2000), 1.

50 Russell M. Nelson, "Protect the Spiritual Power Line," *Ensign*, November 1984, 30.

51 Holland (2000), 203.

52 Truman G. Madsen, *Joseph Smith the Prophet* (Salt Lake City, UT: Bookcraft, 1989), 125.

53 F. Burton Howard, *Marion G. Romney: His Life and Faith* (Salt Lake City: UT; Bookcraft, 1988), 144.

54 Adapted from material presented in Dennis Rainey, *Lonely Husbands, Lonely Wives: Rekindling Intimacy in Every Marriage* (Dallas, TX: Word Publishing, 1989), 5–6.

55 Bruce R. McConkie, *Doctrinal New Testament Commentary*, three volumes (Salt Lake City, UT: Bookcraft, 1987–1988), 2:322, italics added.

56 Spencer J. Condie, *Russell M. Nelson: Father, Surgeon, Apostle* (Salt Lake City, UT: Deseret Book, 2003) 133–34.

57 Dieter F. Uchtdorf, "Of Things That Matter Most," *Ensign*, November 2010, 20–22.

58 Heidi S. Swinton, *To The Rescue: The Biography of Thomas S. Monson* (Salt Lake City, UT: Deseret Book, 2010) 112.

59 Ann M. Dibb, "My Father is a Prophet," *Brigham Young University–Idaho Devotional*, February 19, 2008.

60 Thomas S. Monson, "What Have I Done for Someone Today?" *Ensign*, November 2009, 85.

61   Dallin H. Oaks, "Good, Better, Best," *Ensign*, November 2007, 104–8.

62   Dallin H. Oaks, "Good, Better, Best," 105.

63   See Richard G. Scott, "To Have Peace and Happiness," *CES Fireside for Young Adults*, September 12, 2010.

64   Neal A. Maxwell, *Deposition of a Disciple* (Salt Lake City, UT; Deseret Book, 1976), 58.

65   Stephen Covey, *The Seven Habits of Highly Successful People* (New York, NY: Free Press, 1989), 161.

66   Aspen Books, compiler, *LDS Speaker's Sourcebook* (Salt Lake City, UT: Aspen Books, 1991), 529.

67   Marvin J. Ashton, "We Serve That Which We Love," *Ensign*, May 1981, 23–24.

68   Ezra Taft Benson, *The Teachings of Ezra Taft Benson* (Salt Lake City, UT: Bookcraft, 1998), 391.

69   Neal A. Maxwell, *The Neal A. Maxwell Quote Book*, Cory H. Maxwell, compiler (Salt Lake City, UT: Bookcraft, 1997), 25.

70   Lucile C. Tate, *Boyd K. Packer: A Watchman on the Tower* (Salt Lake City, UT: Bookcraft, 1995), 74–75.

71   Hinckley, *Glimpses*, Virginia H. Pearce, editor (Salt Lake City, UT: Deseret Book, 1999), 42–43.

72   Spencer W. Kimball, "The False Gods We Worship," *Ensign*, June 1976, 4–5.

73   Dallin H. Oaks, "Spirituality," *Ensign*, November 1985, 62.

74   James E. Faust, "The Abundant Life," *Ensign*, November 1985, 8.

75   Joseph Smith, *Teachings of the Prophet Joseph Smith*, Joseph

Fielding Smith, compiler (Salt Lake City, UT: Deseret Book, 1976), 91.

76   Richard G. Scott, "To Have Peace and Happiness," *CES Fireside for Young Adults*, September 12, 2012, Brigham Young University.

77   Thomas G. Alexander, *Things in Heaven and Earth – The Life and Times of Wilford Woodruff, A Mormon Prophet* (Salt Lake City, UT: Signature Books, 1993), 231. See also Journal History, October 7, 1896, where we find a record of the details of President Woodruff's encounter.

78   Ezra Taft Benson, "A Sacred Responsibility," *Ensign*, May 1986, 78.

79   Gordon B. Hinckley, "Of Missions, Temples, and Stewardship," *Ensign*, November 1995, 53.

80   Richard G. Scott, *Finding Peace, Happiness, and Joy* (Salt Lake City, UT: Deseret Book, 2007), 287.

81   *Deseret News*, Church Section, December 12, 1936, volume 344, number 61, cited in Margie Calhoun, *Stories of Insight and Inspiration*, second edition (Salt Lake City, UT: Bountiful Press, 1993), 287–88.

82   The story of their struggles and success is told in the 2000 movie *Remember the Titans*.

83   Hinckley, *Glimpses*, 191.

84   Dew, *Go Forward with Faith*, 440.

85   Marion D. Hanks, "Eternal Marriage," *Ensign*, November 1984, 37.

86   Leslie F. Church, editor, *The NIV Matthew Henry Commentary, In One Volume* (Grand Rapids, MI: Zondervan, 1992), 7.

87 Bruce R. McConkie, "Christ and the Creation," in Mark L. McConkie, editor, *Doctrines of the Restoration: Sermons and Writings of Bruce R. McConkie* (Salt Lake City, UT: Bookcraft, 1989), 190.

88 Edward L. Kimball & Andrew E. Kimball, Jr., *Spencer W. Kimball: Twelfth President of The Church of Jesus Christ of Latter-day Saints* (Salt Lake City, UT: Bookcraft, 1977), 115.

89 Lavina Fielding Anderson, "Dallin H. Oaks," *Ensign*, April 1981, 37.

Index

About the Authors

ALONZO L. GASKILL IS A professor of Church history and doctrine at Brigham Young University. He holds a bachelors degree in philosophy, a masters in theology, and a PhD in biblical studies. Brother Gaskill has taught at BYU since 2003. Prior to coming to BYU, he served in a variety of assignments within the Church Educational System—most recently as the director of the LDS Institute of Religion at Stanford University (1995–2003).

STEVEN T. LINFORD IS THE director of the Orem University Institute adjacent to Utah Valley University. He also works for programs such as Especially for Youth and BYU Campus Education Week. He served in the Italy Milan Mission and has served as a bishop, high councilor, and counselor in a BYU stake presidency. He received a BA from the University of Utah, a MEd from Utah State, and a PhD

in family studies from Brigham Young University. Steve and his wife, Melanie, are the parents of three children and a new beautiful granddaughter.